LAND
GIRLS

For all former land girls

LAND GIRLS

Women's Voices from the
Wartime Farm

JOAN
MANT

AMBERLEY

This edition first published 2012

Amberley Publishing
The Hill, Stroud
Gloucestershire, GL5 4EP

www.amberleybooks.com

Copyright © Joan Mant 2009, 2012

The right of Joan Mant to be identified as the Author
of this work has been asserted in accordance with the
Copyrights, Designs and Patents Act 1988.

British Library Cataloguing in Publication Data.
A catalogue record for this book is available from the British Library.

ISBN 978 1 4456 1048 1

Typesetting and origination by Amberley Publishing
Printed in Great Britain

CONTENTS

INTRODUCTION:
THE WOMEN'S LAND ARMY

By the Spring of 1939 when the increased need for agricultural workers had been foreseen there had already been a trial run for a Women's Land Army. The WLA was created in 1917 and by 1918 23,000 had been enrolled. By September 1939 there were already 1,000 volunteers and by December 4,544.

However, these figures seem puny when measured by the estimated deficit in March 1940 of 102,000 regular and 30,000 seasonal workers. Substitute workers, i.e. the WLA, gang labour, roadmen, conscientious objectors, refugees, industrial unemployed, children etc. were insufficient to fill the gap. Of these the continuously increasing source of labour was the Women's Land Army, overcoming prejudice by sheer hard work and determination. In January 1942 recruitment had been speeded up by the policy which made women liable to direction by the Ministry of Labour.

Although the WLA was part of the Ministry of Agriculture and Fisheries, it was entirely staffed and run by women, the Hon. Director being Lady Denman DBE, whose home, Balcombe Place, was given over as general headquarters. From here spread a network of regional officers, county organising secretaries, district representatives and finally the land girls themselves.

For the land girl, of course, the most important of these was the representative, the visible face of the hierarchy, who was responsible for her welfare and who should have visited her once a month and sent in a detailed report. The girl who had a good representative, or knew how to contact her, was fortunate indeed.

In the appendix to *Women Who Went to War 1938–46* by Eric Taylor, a note read: 'Never before had women undertaken so many varied tasks in the country's defence. Thousands joined the three highly organised military Services—the WRNS, ATS and WAAF. Others performed important work in industry in order to release men to active service.' Well, we too went to war and here are stories from some of the many who replied to pleas in their local newspaper, or who heard the comedian, Charlie Chester's programme asking them to contact me.

PART ONE

I

THE VANGUARD—WORLD WAR I

Those of us who joined the WLA from 1939 on were not the pioneers perhaps we thought we were. That accolade truly belongs to those in the First World War who enlisted in the newly formed Women's Land Army. Like us, later on, they came from all backgrounds for all reasons. Jessica Godwin, for instance, says:

'I was a lady's companion (a very dull life!) and was glad of a real excuse to leave.'

Clara Sibley had already been doing 'war work' at Woolwich Arsenal on nights machining cordite bags and decided to join the Forestry Corps after hearing from her sister what a lovely life it was. Phyllis Collyer left boarding school at Eastbourne just before Easter 1918 and, wanting to do war work and loving the outdoor life, joined the WLA. When I commented on the boots Phyllis was wearing in the wartime photograph she sent to me, she said:

'They were very comfortable indeed but you had to allow ten minutes to get them on.'

She remembers that she and her sister lived at the farm, earning £1 2s 0d a week, fifteen shillings of which went to the farmer's wife for their keep:

'The cowman, my sister and I started milking eight cows at 6 a.m. by hand, with a lantern for light.'

Listen to M. Price:

'In those days it was the rich and the poor, no choice, so I took cookery lessons on leaving school. I was the middle one of three in the kitchen of a wealthy family. They were nice people but with the coming of rationing it was uninteresting so I decided the country was the job for me. I did four years in the Land Army... 12 hours a day, £1 a week, 15/- kept back for our keep. No machines. I did general farm work, then to a flax camp... the first aeroplane wings were made from flax. My next trip was to Lincolnshire picking up potatoes, when the Zeppelins were over. From there to Kent for threshing, where I was ill, and after that to Somerset and milking twice a day, including Sundays... half dark and half asleep I got along to the farm, picked up my stool and pail, not knowing the old cowman had brought in a young bull—you can guess what happened. I found myself the other side on the ground. I don't think I had better tell you what the farmer said!'

Clara Sibley, who joined the Forestry Corps as it was then, says:

'It was lovely out in the forest all day. I was on a farm at Chelgrove and the farmer used to pack us up with a bottle of milk each and a load of sandwiches. Our job was cutting down trees for pit props. One day when we left the forest to go home we had to go through a field full of bulls waiting at the gate we wanted to go through, so back we went the long way round and when we told the farmer he was very amused. He said, "They be only three years old me dears," but that seemed old enough for us.'

M. Price remembers too that she was a bridesmaid in her uniform when a fellow land girl married.

Jessica Godwin gives a vivid picture of her life then:

'I joined the Land Army at the end of June 1917 and was sent with another girl, Jane, who joined with me, to a farm at a place called Sutton Green about four miles from Guildford. When we got to the farm, there were already two girls and we were lodged in a cottage and looked after by a young woman with a small boy about three years old (who cut up all the sheets on our beds!). We received eighteen shillings a week and out of this we paid the woman fifteen shillings a week for our board and lodging. Of course she was paid to look after us and she did it very badly indeed. It was a dairy farm and we had to bring the cows in at 6 a.m. in the morning. We two new girls had to practise on a rubber udder filled with water, but at the end of a week we were allowed to milk a cow; when all the cows were milked (by hand) there was the dairy to clean out and how we hurried the cows out before they dropped their "pancakes"! Besides the cows there were chicken and geese and calves to feed and chicken houses to clean out. The farmer had only one oldish man and a boy besides we girls; the man, Packer, had a very lovely singing voice and would sing while we cleaned out ditches and what an amazing lot of muck there was to clean out!

We went back to the cottage at 8 o'clock for breakfast and at 1 o'clock for dinner, at 4 o'clock we brought the cows in again for milking and all was done by 6 o'clock when we went home for a high tea, but the woman was a terribly bad housekeeper and we were very hungry.

We were not allowed to have hairpins in our hair in case they dropped out and the cows swallowed them, so we wore our hair in a plait down our backs. Mine was much admired as it was below my waist and a rich chestnut colour. It was nice to be admired for something as I have been told I was very plain.

Jane and I asked if we could join the tractor section. We had two gentlemen come over from America with the first Fordson tractor brought to England, Fordson No. 1, and they showed how to drive it. They stayed for a few days and then our master mechanic, Harries, took over and taught us. He took the engine apart and we watched him put it together again; we could do our own simple repairs and at the end of six weeks we were trained! We were to get 30/- a week in wages and a shilling extra for every acre we ploughed, 4d for cultivating and 4d per acre for corn cutting...

The Fordson tractors we drove in those days were quite different from the present day tractors, ours had iron wheels with spikes on them and when we went on the road we had to screw on iron bands. We had to start them with a crank handle, no self-starter and no brakes. We started them with a little petrol in the commutator and switched over quickly to paraffin.

The first field I ploughed was an 18-acre one and I did it in a week. The farmer was most excited. I *think* a man with a two-horse plough used to plough half an acre a day.'

2

WHY DID WE DO IT?

What a mixed bunch we were! Any army, volunteer or conscript, is made up of people from all parts of the country and from widely differing backgrounds. The WLA was no exception.

For some the war came as an interruption to studies, an interruption which became permanent. Elinor Grant was training to become a dietician, Norah Hawkes was at a domestic science college but on the outbreak of war found no opening for cookery demonstrations. Marjorie James had become a part-time music student at the Manchester College of Music and volunteered for the WLA in case she was drafted into munitions.

We came from offices, shops ranging from the Co-op to Harrods; libraries, including Leeds, Hackney and even the Bodleian, gave up their young staff; hairdressers, machinists and barmaids all took to the land. Comparatively few of us had much knowledge of the 'Great Outdoors' and as one girl put it 'A.G. Street [popular writer and broadcaster on rural themes] had a lot to answer for'.*

One difference between the WLA and the women's forces was that girls were accepted at 17½ years of age instead of 18 years, and at that age a six months' wait to do one's bit was just too long if there was a good alternative.

Jean Dawe sums it up:

'I left school and went into hairdressing... By that time I was 17 and... the only service taking girls under 18 was the WLA.'

Or how about the sheer determination to join the WLA shown by Jean Doe, who had tasted country living whilst an evacuee and knew it was for her.

'I "lost" my identity card, defaced my ration book, and joined up at 16. I was very shy.'

Joan Law is quite succinct:

'It was 1943 when I joined the Land Army at the ripe old age of 17½, as green as a hornet, determined to do my bit.'

Another factor leading to enlistment in the WLA was parental prejudice against the other women's forces. As M. Woodcraft says:

'Before I joined the Land Army I was a secretary in a Court photographers in the West End. At that time I was living in Ilford on the outskirts of London. I can't say the Land Army was my first choice—I wanted to go into one of the women's services but I was still young enough to take notice of my father's remarks who had just been called up for the Air Force. He preferred the Land Army so that was that.'

Jo Bicknells' young husband had said:

'It's no good you going into the forces—you'd be in the glasshouse all the time!'

Well, we didn't have a glasshouse in the WLA but we certainly had hard labour. Joy Lawrence was in domestic service at Alkham vicarage:

'I wanted to get away from domineering parents but to mention joining the ATS, WRNS or WAAF was frowned on and severely criticised so I decided to join the Land Army, said nothing to no-one until I had been accepted and had my medical... When my date to join arrived, I told my parents and this wasn't right either, the farms in Kent were not of the right standards etc. but the vicar wished me luck and said he was sorry I was leaving.'

May Readey was 19 years old, working in a safe job in a glove factory and doing firewatching on a regular basis, but she was bored:

'I wanted to join the ATS but my parents were most upset as I already had two brothers in the army. I reasoned that my parents could hardly worry about me working on a farm and so I sent for details of the WLA. My posting was to Wheathill Farm near Dorrington, Shropshire. I remember so well the Saturday of July 1942 sitting on the deserted railway station at Dorrington waiting for the porter-cum-stationmaster to close the booking office and show me the way to the farm. He put my luggage on his bike and off we set. It was only when I got to know the locality that I realised how far out of his way we had come.'

Julia Porteous was chargehand in a grocer's small shop:

'When I got my call-up papers it was for the WRNS and I passed my medical and was to be a stewardess, but as my father was a naval driver he saw what the stewardesses had to do and said I would be better running after the animals, so they gave me the choice of the WLA.'

Marjorie Rossi, aged 17½, was a junior shorthand-typist working in Leeds. She had always hated the idea of working in an office in a city and always wanted to work on a farm.

'Before the war this was nonsense as far as my parents were concerned, however I had a row with my mother and during my lunch hour at the office I went to the recruiting office and got the necessary forms but was told as I was under age I would need my parents' permission. That night I filled the forms in and left them on the kitchen table. My mother said, "Well, now she's a sensible girl", so I was in.'

Theo Rice worked for a chartered accountant in Chancery Lane, London, when she decided to contribute to the war effort:

'I planned with a school friend to join the WRNS. However, my father and elder brother put paid to that idea so I joined my cousin Bette who was already in the Land Army.'

Kathleen Ellis:

'From the perfumery department to a cowshed was certainly a change, but I knew I wouldn't stay as a shop assistant and that I would have to do some kind of war work. My boyfriend, who was an engineer co-pilot on Halifaxes, barred me from joining the forces, and in those days I did as he said, so I didn't think he would object to the Land Army and I joined. My mother and father were horrified as I had never been away from home before, and when my posting came through to go to Woodstock, near Oxford, I'm sure my mother thought it was outer Mongolia.'

Vera Wix too was thwarted by her father:

'Really wanted to go in the WAAFs or ATS, changed the date on cards to apply with a cousin of mine six months my junior. Somehow, however, father found out and reported us. The only way we were told was to join the WLA as younger girls were taken. My mother said, "You will never be any good".'

Some seemed to have joined whilst looking the other way. Daphne Blanford, for instance, says:

'The WLA recruiting office was just round the corner from Smith Square where

I worked in an advertising agency. I enrolled on impulse; my friends and colleagues thought I was mad and predicted an early return to town life. It was seven years before I returned but never again to live in London.'

Amy Johnstone too, seems to have made a spur of the moment decision:

'I was 25 when war broke out, holding a good job as a buffet barmaid in one of Aberdeen's better hotels. Life was good, life was fun! I enjoyed my job, we had some very important people passing through, theatre folks, sporting numbers, even on occasion, royalty. I had my own little flat and good friends—oh yes, a few of the boys went off, we had blackouts, then the bombs fell now and then, we weren't frightened but it sobered us!

One fine sunny afternoon a friend, a nurse, and I were walking up a street when there in a shop window was a display of uniforms for all the women's services. My friend said, "That's it! We'll join the Land Army", and there and then we walked down to the office and signed on the dotted line; we were, in a way, country girls as we had both spent our childhood in the country. We had such plans! Well, in a couple of days my boss was notified, oh, he certainly begged me to think again but, as I would be called up soon, he wished me luck. An hour later my friend phoned, she had just been on the carpet before Matron, in no way would she get away. Yes, I did weep then and regretted what I had done!'

Yet another spur to joining was the thought that conscription would make us do something for which we had no wish. Office worker Olga Tremayne sums it up:

'I thought that perhaps I should volunteer in case I was drafted to a service which I wouldn't choose. I chose the Land Army.'

Others waited for call-up. Sheila McWilliam for instance:

'...came from Ballater where I was born and brought up and I was the eldest of eight so had to work away from home when I was 13. I was in domestic service then and stayed till I was called up. I did get the chance to go to Glasgow to the ammunitions but that life was not for me. I joined the local Timber Corps.'

Enid Bennell saw the Land Army as an escape:

'I left school at 14 and went straight into service. It was a boarding house on the seafront at Southend. I was the only domestic so it was slogging from morning to night for a pound a month and a couple of hours off on Sundays. Then I did a stint

in a convent. Apart from dodging chapel those nuns chased us round, that sure
was a penance. Then it was the Land Army.'

Pique played a part in Chris Breeze's transformation into a land girl:

'I was 18. I asked my boss for a rise, as I was only getting 29/- a week, and my
mother becoming a widow was only receiving 10/-. All he gave me was a shilling,
so off I went in my tea-break and signed on.'

Anger drove Barbara Youngman:

'My father had been killed in a London air raid and I was so angry. Only being
17 years old the Services wouldn't have me so I went for the WLA.'

Joyce Palmer, too, decided that enough was enough:

'I was a sales assistant in St Paul's churchyard. In view of the persistent bombing
and the difficulty of getting to work from where I lived, which was near the Isle of
Dogs, and being attacked round the clock, my firm had accommodation and an
excellent shelter so I went and lived in. For safety I took most of my clothes and
treasured things. On the night of 29th December 1940, the Luftwaffe decided to
set us all alight. My firm caught fire and we were all evacuated into the crypt of St
Paul's where we stayed until the All Clear. My case with all my things in, ready to
grab in case of an emergency, was completely forgotten in panic. Having decided
enough was enough and only having the clothes I stood up in, I went and joined
the WLA.'

Joining the WLA was sometimes second best. Elsie Druce joined up at 18,
before call-up. As she says:

'I did not fancy the regimentation of the other forces (although I did have a
desire to be a WREN and sail around some harbour delivering mail to sailors).'

Connie McNichol, too, had other plans:

'I thought I would like to do something other than be in an office and got permission
to be released for other service. I actually tried to join the WAAF but all they required
early in 1942 were cooks and barrage balloon operators and weighing in at 6st. 10lb, I
didn't think I would be very suitable for these jobs. I therefore decided to join the Land
Army and no sooner had I done so than the WAAF lists were opened for all sorts of
occupations.'

Dorothy Harmer had worked in a grocers weighing up rations and counting coupons:

'I didn't want to join the WLA but when I got to the Labour Exchange they weren't taking any more recuits for the WRNS, WAAF or ATS in that order and the girl behind the desk said what about the WLA? Boy was I green! I had no idea what the job entailed.'

And so it was with most of us.

When L. Shepherd was nearly 18 she tried to join the WAAFs but at the time they only wanted chiropodist orderlies:

'We came out of the recruitment centre and automatically joined another queue which turned out to be the Land Army.'

Olive Pettitt also seemed to go on the land by accident:

'I worked in a drapery shop. One lunch-time my friend and I were wandering round the town when we passed a building with posters about the WLA. We went in just to have a look. Ten minutes later out we came, both signed up to work on a dairy farm. Then the awful business to tell the manager of the shop what we had done. It took us three whole days to tell him... He was furious and ignored us for the three weeks we were there.'

Some girls turned to the Land Army when they failed the forces' medical. M. Griffin could not get into the WAAF on health grounds but found she was accepted by the WLA. Jo Greatorex's sight precluded her from the other women's forces but the WLA welcomed her, and Jean Oglethorpe says:

'I was a typist at the time. I actually volunteered for the WRNS and WAAFs first, but was turned down owing to foot deformities! Then, the WLA accepted me—feet and all, and put me in boots, and my feet got a real bashing.'

Others, like Doris Rowland, had the Land Army thrust upon them:

'I was working with one other girl in service for a vicar and his wife in Canterbury. In the summer of 1940 we were informed by the vicar's wife that they were moving to a smaller house and would have no further need for our services, so she had enrolled us both in the WLA. We had "lived in" at the vicarage and our wages had been 14/- per week.'

Branwen Weekes, with a friend, decided to opt for horticulture:

'She said it sounded more ladylike than agriculture. I'm not sure that we even knew the difference. I was a civil servant in what was then the Welsh Board of Health and by the end of 1941 it had become clear that I was not indispensable and that I could expect my call-up papers any day. For some reason I didn't fancy the forces at all. Perhaps it was just as well. I've turned out to be a rather bossy woman and a couple of stripes in the army might have transformed me into something thoroughly unpleasant. So I decided to volunteer for the Women's Land Army; never in my life having sown so much as a packet of seeds here was virgin soil indeed.

The next step was the medical examination and for this I was sent to a most formidable woman in Penylan. After going through the usual routine she held a watch to my ear and asked me to say when I could no longer hear it ticking. I was terrified as she moved it slowly away because I could hear nothing and was quite clearly going to be classified as deaf. I guessed the distance to be about an arm's length away and her look of scorn and displeasure still haunts me. The watch was not going.'

Daphne Stone had offered her services to the WLA before war broke out:

'...so during the days that followed the sound of the first siren it was rather an anti-climax to find oneself still awaiting the official call to action. I later realised that the delay was due (1) to the fact that girls were to begin with only required to replace men who had been called up and (2) unlike the other services who were under the dircction of the War Office, we were to be selected and supervised by officials of local county headquarters, many of whom were not part of the farming community, nor even mildly interested in it, which was to prove most disconcerting when the need for complaint or arbitration arose.'

This last point, I am sure, was the reason so many square pegs ended up in round holes and had to stay there.

Joyce Whiteley, too, wanted to have some choice in her call-up:

'Not fancying the disciplines of the ATS, nor the Air Force equivalent, the WAAF, and thinking it unlikely that I would be able to get into the much sought-after WRNS, I opted for the Women's Land Army. I asked to join the Timber Corps rather liking the idea of bringing on little shoots in a nursery greenhouse. Someone had told me this was what they did in the Timber Corps! The uniform was the same as the WLA wore except that the headgear was a green beret which I thought much more attractive than the brimmed pudding basin khaki felt hat that the public were used to seeing.'

Yvonne Timbs, now in Australia, lived in Fulwell, Sunderland, and had no contact with rural life:

> 'After leaving school I worked briefly as a cashier and then worked in Woolworths and made friends with three other girls there. When war started we realised we had to join a service so picked the Land Army as it was different and the least regimented. Not very patriotic were we?'

When Gladys Levingbird was 18 she received call-up papers which meant that she had to go into the forces, or a munitions factory.

> 'I was working at the time in a wholesale stationery firm, which was a small family concern and I had been there since leaving school at 14. Each time that I received these papers my employer would give me a letter requesting a deferment... I wanted to go into the Land Army, so I asked if they would refuse deferment, but not let it be known to my employer that I had requested this. I wanted to be loyal to my firm, but the feeling to go into the Land Army was stronger.

Maude Milliss was a 20-year-old shorthand-typist in 1943:

> 'The only other choice open to me was the brickworks! Being rather shy and reserved I did not want to join any of the women's services, so I opted for the open-air life, much to the surprise of my family as I hated the cold weather and suffered terribly from chilblains every winter (surprisingly I had very few while working on the land).'

A picture begins to emerge of the future land girl, a rebel perhaps, impulsive, not keen on regimentation, sometimes running from rather than to, but most of them with the greatest gift of all—a sense of humour.

3

INTERVIEWS

It was not enough, however, to opt for the WLA; there was an interview first and then a medical. The interviews were somewhat idiosyncratic, although I imagine the interviewers were trying to make sure we knew what we were getting into. (I wonder if they themselves knew?)

I remember facing a very 'county' lady across a table as she said, 'Do you realise how vile it will be?' I untruthfully replied, 'Yes,' (well, I would, wouldn't I?)—and I was in. My medical took the form of a visit to my own doctor (who hadn't seen me for years), who said, 'That's a good idea, do you the world of good,' and signed the certificate without even asking me to take my hat off. Yes, we wore hats then.

Andrey Wiitta's interviewer asked first what her height was and proceeded to measure her. When it was found that Audrey was 4ft. 11¾ins it was, 'Sorry, you have to be 5ft.' Drawing herself to her full height (now there's a thought) Audrey replied, 'All right, then I won't do anything.' Perhaps feeling that England couldn't manage without such material the interviewer decided, 'Oh well, all right then,' and here was another recruit. Asked about her shoe size Audrey said, 'Three.' 'Sorry, only fives,' came the answer. And size fives in shoes and boots she had.

Vera Redshaw remembers:

'When I was interviewed by the WLA Committee I said I would like to do general farming but as I was only about 5ft. 3ins and very slight they eyed me as if I were the runt of a litter of pigs and expressed doubt about my ability to cope. However, on consulting my medical report they decided I might survive.'

L. Shepherd, too, was very slight and says:

'At that time I was half the size I am now and the interviewer said to me, "You have a very puny chest," and I replied with gusto, "Is that what one has to work with, one's chest?" She was so taken aback that she accepted me.'

Perhaps the interviewer recognised guts as well as gusto!

Phyllis Munn says:

'It was with some misgivings that I presented myself at the nearest WLA recruiting office, but not without good reason, as I soon discovered. When I pushed open the door I very nearly panicked and withdrew, for seated inside were three girls of about my age, but there the similarity ended. They were all blessed with well-developed figures and looked extremely tough, while I barely passed the five-foot mark, and there was no disguising that I was one of the lean kind. It was clear that these ladies would not be disturbed by any farm task with which they might be confronted... I thought I detected a look of tolerant amusement on their faces as three pairs of eyes turned in my direction... I came through successfully, my unpromising appearance apparently being of no significance.'

It wasn't only size which must have made some of us seem very unlikely recruits. Joan Hawell, for instance, had obtained a job at Lachasse in Berkeley Square, the designer being the well-known Hardy Amies:

'By the age of 19 years, although by now a key worker at Lachasse (screened from call-up to keep the business surviving) I had made up my mind to join the WLA. I enrolled at Victoria. The lady in charge looked at me long and hard. I recall I must have looked like a model from Vogue, complete with a veil on my hat. She did her best to convince me I would be better suited making uniforms with my skills, but I was not being put off at this stage. I signed all that was required and became a land girl. I would have liked to have presented myself to her a few months later in welly boots shrouded in cow dung.'

Marie Brockett too, arrived for an interview looking very unlike a daughter of the soil:

'The WLA seemed a good idea, so I wended my way up to HQ in London and attempted to enrol. As I was wearing a perky hat and probably looking everything a country girl would not, the lady who interviewed me expounded all the bad side of the work and advised me to go home and think again! This stung me somewhat and after arriving home I got on my bike and went to see a local farmer... who offered me a job with his dairy herd—I received my uniform by return.'

Jean Dawe also remembers her interview, in this instance with the Hon. Mrs Bathurst:

'She took one look at me, smartly dressed, nails polished and hair newly set and said, "You realise you will be dressed in dungarees and gum boots cleaning out cowsheds etc. don't you?" I think she thought I wouldn't stick it for long but I did, though it was very hard and dirty work.'

Joy Eichler, however, has the last word:

'...passed the medical but was only asked if I had flat feet or varicose veins.'

4

UNIFORM

The dictionary has two definitions for 'uniform', one is 'distinctive clothing intended to identify the wearer as a member of a certain organisation or group'—well, we were certainly identifiable. The second definition is 'always the same, not varying'— oh dear!

Some joined the WLA because of the uniform, others in spite of it. Some girls were measured and fitted, the rest of us had to take what was available on a hit or miss basis—and it showed. The curate's egg had nothing on us! Gwen Lawrence, for instance, had no uniform at the beginning:

'...so I had my tennis shorts and shirt, and by the end of the first day I looked like a well manured sheep!'

The greatcoats, when they arrived, were splendid, comfortable and hardwearing on the lines of a British Warm. They were not, however, issued immediately on enlistment but came later presumably because of the likelihood of some of the volunteers leaving the service and taking their overcoats with them. This was hard lines on those who joined in winter time but as well as not wishing to be regimented, the WLA girls could be self-assertive, as Dorothy Harmer says:

'... about ten of us thumbed a lift to Durham City where the uniforms were and demanded overcoats or we wouldn't work. We got them!'

Mabel Williams, too, comments on the cold:

'There were about 40 girls, all raw recruits, all in uniform, but there was a shortage of overcoats, and as it was February we were all very cold. Then the conversation started as to how many jumpers we each had under our green "issue" jumpers—and that green jumper was the only one with which we were issued.'

Vivienne Passmore became battle scarred:

'The first winter proved to be a very hard one, and owing to the temporary inadequacy of the uniform I soon had chilblains on most awkward places owing to ditching in freezing water.'

In her book, Sackville-West quotes a friend of hers saying we looked like 'guys' with our uniforms being mixed with 'civvies', and hats at all angles. From our point of view our uniform issue was good, of superb quality, but insufficient and we had to supplement it and make adjustments. We had two aertex shirts and I was able to buy a second-hand one for 1/6d, otherwise I wore pre-war blouses. We seemed to go through our two pairs of woolly socks at an alarming rate; we had two pairs of dungarees but if one pair was in the wash and, wearing the second pair, we stood at the wrong end of a cow when she coughed...

Naturally, we overcame our difficulties and Doreen Liebrandt made superb efforts:

'I was always proud of my uniform but sometimes used to cheat to improve the look of it. Those aertex shirts were useless with a tie so I had an Army officer's khaki cotton shirt which went much better with our gaberdine dress breeches. I always got a size larger than necessary and had it altered for a better fit. I kept these for walking-out dress. One thing I would like to stress is that we wore breeches *not* jodhpurs as I have often heard and read since. With the dungarees in the summer we were wearing "hotpants" long before the sixties!

I always wore my felt hat as a trilby, steaming it to make it hold its shape.'

Audrey Bagnall too, made adjustments:

'Although the Land Army uniform was standard, girls soon put their own touches to what they wore. Any discarded old pullovers, cut out the sleeves, with a minimum of stitching, you had an extra pair of socks to go in your wellingtons. If the remaining body part was any good, you could wear it back to front, under your working pullover. That was a lot warmer and saved wearing a shirt. By the time I had been in the Land Army six months my breeches were dyed dark brown.

Then there was "the hat"; that gave scope for individuality. I can remember a very happy evening in the kitchen at Limpsfield steaming our hats, we got more shapes out of those basic felt hats than one would think possible. My hat ended up like a "cowboy" hat with the backbrim steamed up and the front brim steamed down, my badge pinned centre front. Best of all I had a long thin brown leather bootlace, a few stitches fastened each end of this to each side of my hat, near the ear, with a wooden woggle I could fasten my hat under my chin or drop it behind my head. I was quite pleased with the end results and always wore my hat at a jaunty angle when I went "out", as if it were a Paris model.'

The hats, however, were very much disliked in their original state. When Audrey Wiitta, for instance, tried on her uniform and put on the hat her family fell about and told her she looked like a frog under a dock leaf.

Footwear too caused a difficulty if our feet didn't fit the shoes or boots with which we were issued. I had a pair of black army boots, so big I'm sure I could have done an about turn in them leaving the boots standing still. I. Pamphlett too, was shaken by the footwear:

> 'When I saw the boots and hard leather shoes I knew my poor feet were in for it. Still, I liked myself in the walking out uniform, and I put the hat on the back of my head and thought I looked great.'

Our wellingtons were worn stuffed usually with dad's socks, or hay. Our families were wonderful, providing us with 'passed on' gloves, socks and jerseys to supplement our issue. Elsie Druce was very fortunate:

> 'Our uniform was of the finest quality except for the boots which were very hard. Our shepherd soon sorted them out. He took us into the barn, where hanging from the roof we saw large sacks full of sheep wool. We were hoisted into the sacks wearing the boots and told to tread. After a while when we got down the boots were as soft as silk and really waterproofed.'

Audrey Sykes found her lace-up boots comfortable but not entirely waterproof:

> 'I remember standing a pair on the kitchen boiler to dry and burning a hole right through the sole! We wore corduroy breeches and thick socks in the winter and khaki dungarees in the summer, aertex shirts and green wool jumpers. The hats were appalling and everyone loathed them, we never wore them unless at some function, they were deep crowned and wide brimmed. The forestry girls came off better with green berets.'

The breeches were warm and, if they fitted, good to work in, though not for milking for which the dungarees with a milking coat were best. Spilt milk, or milk that missed the bucket and ended up on our legs soon began to smell. Vera Gaskell explained:

> '...wearing the uniform which was much too big—I was still growing. The cords stuck out at my hips like wings and I'm sure I deserved a medal just for riding on the bus wearing them, not to mention the cowboy hat and stiff black boots.'

Maisie Geraerts, too, remembers:

'... the uniforms were enormous and I had to take my breeches in two inches all round. They hadn't any size three shoes so I had to wait for them, the boots were all right with two pairs of socks.'

Theo Rice's introduction to the uniform was despair:

'The breeches insisted on standing up when I wanted to sit down and it was impossible to work in them in comfort (I was the wrong shape!). I favoured the dungarees, the pockets being heaven sent, large, and in the right place in which to put my hands and thrust my fists into my stomach to alleviate the monthly pain.'

Kathleen Ellis felt disbelief when her uniform arrived:

'I didn't know whether to laugh or cry. A dressmaker my mother knew very kindly did some alterations and I looked passable, except for the hat, and you couldn't do much with that.'

Marjorie Harvey felt that the most important statistic when trying on a uniform was height:

'Being of stock size and weight I did quite well uniform-wise but my friend, although being the same weight, was tall and thin and therefore the breeches hung in folds giving the appearance of a saggy elephant. It is surprising, however, what can be achieved with a sewing machine and they were soon licked into shape... our most popular forms of apparel were the cool aertex blouses, green sweaters and dungarees. In the summer our breeches were hacked off well above the knee to become not the most elegant of shorts. Our stout shoes weighed a ton but were most comfortable when "broken in" and our feet had become adjusted to them after court shoes and we rarely suffered from aching feet, although we were on them most of the day.'

Joan Clifford remembers receiving the first instalment of her uniform which:

'...was two short-sleeved shirts, one green pullover, two pairs of socks, one pair of shoes, one bib and brace overall, a hat, a pair of rubber boots and a very long, thin mac which came down to my ankles. This was in November! We had to give up most of our clothing coupons, but always had to supply all our own underclothes. I had the rest of my uniform during the next six months, including a greatcoat and a pair of breeches, and I was able to buy some second-hand uniform over the years from the Oxford WLA office.'

Marion Powell, too found difficulties with fit:

'...being tall I needed the largest sizes which needed lots of taking in as I'm not very fat. Old breeches always got cut off at the knees to make shorts and then dyed either green or maroon.'

Mabel Potter also went in for changing the look of things:

'One of the girls one day put a spot of bleach in the water when washing her fawn aertex blouse and it came out a lovely shade of yellow so we all followed suit and the secretary blew her top when she saw us all in yellow shirts!'

Margaret Bodman was without wellingtons for a long time but found:

'Boots and gaiters most useful. Variety of materials and warmth of breeches. No necessary scarf issued. Had to supplement with own clothes. Second-hand could be bought later. Had studs put in shoes to make them last.'

Daphne Stone found the benefit of a sense of humour:

'The original felt hat and corduroy breeches were, as most of us found, a laugh, as the former was po-shaped and required kneading into a "pork pie" or perhaps an "Oklahoma" style, whilst the breeches were baggy bloomers only suitable for the more generously proportioned of the girls! Those like myself had to buy our own military style whipcord or jodhpurs for "walking out". The socks provided were also a joke, as the two-pair handout lasted hardly any time at all. I have a letter written to me by our patron at the time, Lady Cornwallis of Kent, congratulating me on gaining a stripe for one year's service, and enclosing a pair of socks. However, it was the thought that counted, wasn't it?'

Betty Otway sums it up:

'Although the issue of uniform was the same for us all, some girls managed to wear it as if it had been tailored specially for them, while the rest of us just got by, cleanliness had nothing to do with it, the tilt of a hat brim, or a neat collar, some girls could look really good in dungarees and gumboots. When things wore out and we applied for replacement, it was quite common to get a size larger or smaller then the size asked for, which was OK for clothes which could be altered a little, but shoes and boots! The greatcoats were "great", lovely and warm in the cold weather. The aim was to try and get two eventually so that one could be worn for work, and one kept for smartness. Hay inside gumboots kept the feet warm. Shoes on soggy ground just came off and stayed in the mud. On summer days we wore short-sleeved shirts and dungarees, the latter cut into shorts if the heat was excessive.'

5

HOW WE LIVED

The great divide in the WLA was between those who were sent to private billets and those who were posted to hostels. The latter worked and lived together, the former on farms or market gardens, sometimes alone or with two or three others.

Some of us were very fortunate and were wonderfully looked after by our landladies, who became our friends. We were young and naive, probably leaving home for the first time, since young girls did not then generally leave home until marriage unless it was to go into domestic service. Sometimes home-sickness could become a health problem, and for most this was also to be our first contact with rural living. If we thought at all about our prospective way of life we probably imagined bucolic bliss and to quote Sackville-West from what was regarded as the official record of the the Land Army, so did she!

> '...a genial kitchen at supper-time, when the white tablecloth is spread under the lamp and the table is set with yellow plates, and there is a huge loaf and a bowl of tomatoes and jade green lettuce in the centre, the fire glows behind the bars of the grate, the kettle bubbles gently. The man of the house sits in his shirt sleeves reading the newspaper while he waits for his tea, the children stare, the dog gets up, the housewife comes out from the scullery wiping her hands, and there is the land girl in the midst of them, young, pretty, healthy, almost like the daughter of the family.'

Fancy that!

Lodging was found for us by our employers or representatives so that we had somewhere to go on first arriving at a farm or market garden. The kindness we met made up for a great deal and some girls remained in touch with their landladies for many years. The kindness Molly Campbell received stays in her memory:

> 'I was billeted for a time with a very kind couple, the husband a cowman. His wife washed the overalls of all the cowmen every week. These were washed in a copper.

Every other Friday the tin bath went the rounds of three cottages and I bathed in an outhouse, the water from the copper still had the suds from the cow-splattered overalls floating on the surface. One evening I heard the husband, who liked to go down to the pub of an evening, shout, "Queenie, where's my clean shirt'?" to which Queenie replied, "If that shirt's good enough to sleep with me in, it's good enough to go down to the pub in." But these people were kindness itself and happily took in a girl from the town, and made me feel quite at home, and cherished, in fact.'

Sometimes the billets were in the farmhouse itself. Marjorie Waterhouse, saying, 'I was so green, childlike—never been away from home before', was one of those who lived on the farm:

'I heard later that the local folk called the farm "that big rough spot". We did not get enough to eat. Our last meal was about 6.30 p.m. after milking and there was not even a drink before bedtime. Each day the farmer's wife gave us tea in a small bottle (a lemonade bottle) which of course was cold when we drank it mid-morning in the field, and two slices of bread and cheese wrapped in newspaper. In the afternoon we had the same out in the field but with jam instead of cheese. We all sat for meals in the kitchen (except Sundays when the farmer, his wife, son Joe and daughter Sue disappeared into the front room for their dinner and tea—I expect they had nicer food than us). The kitchen had a stone floor and a large wooden table (no cloth) and a form at each side. The farmer sat on a chair at the head, and two farm lads, Amy the maid, Joe and Sue, farmer's wife and I sat on the forms. Eight of us. I wondered at first why the farmer's lads ate so quickly but soon found out that if I also did not eat quickly I would get hardly any food, especially at tea-time when just a limited amount of bread was on the plate in the middle!

I needed to send half my wage home each Friday, to help out there. The farmer *did* allow me to finish earlier then so that I could walk the two miles to the village post office for a postal order. One Friday I had just set off when a butcher's van pulled up, gave me a lift to the village and the driver gave me a pork pie, saying, "Here, I know you are half hungered at that farm."

One Sunday afternoon I was out on my own resting in a field under a hedge. The heat and the buzzing of flies must have made me sleepy, I dozed and was late in for tea. The farm lads had eaten theirs and gone off, leaving me one crust of bread. I had nothing more until about 8 a.m. next clay after two hours' work. I dared not ask for more bread. I think I would not have been given any anyhow. Once a Land Army lady, a representative, came to see how I was getting on. She was sent to where I was mowing thistles on my own, using a scythe, in pouring rain. As I did not wish to tell tales I said I was OK. Years later I saw that I should have told the truth.

In a cottage belonging to the farm there were two families—just the women and their children. They had evacuated from Lancashire and sometimes asked me to supper on Sunday evenings (Great!). Although I had eaten my last meal at the farm I had a lovely meal there also. Neither the farmer nor his wife ever said a kind word to me. When the harvest was in I was not needed and in early October was sent to live and work from a hostel named "Merry Thought House" between Penrith and Carlisle.'

In a telephone conversation Eva Briley told how, joining the WLA at 17½ after being a machinist in London, she was the only land girl on the farm, living in the farmhouse. Eva ate with the family but after a meal had to retire to her attic bedroom. She also committed the sin of eventually becoming 18 when her pay would be increased, so the farmer dispensed with her services and took on another 17½-year-old.

Doreen Rapley remembers joining the WLA at 17½ and on her first farm went milking and came to the farmhouse for breakfast which was a cup of tea and a thick slice of fat bacon. When she said she could not manage the bacon the farmer said, 'Perhaps you will at dinner time,' when it was presented again. This lasted for two days before she was finally able to shut her eyes and force it down.

There seems to have been a reservoir of elderly ladies living alone who were willing to have one, or sometimes two, land girls billeted on them. It may have been thought that the land girls were preferable to evacuees but whatever the reason they opened their homes to us in spite of our obvious drawbacks, that is being very hungry after a day working in the open air, and arriving home dirty, sometimes muddy and smelly, and needing hot water and feeding.

For a time I lived with a Junoesque spinster who had a penchant for paste sandwiches, and those of us working at that particular market garden would peer at our lunchtime 'piece' and swap them round a bit so that Joan didn't always have paste, and Roma could have a change from lettuce. Eventually I found another billet so that I could be part of a family with laughter, good food and companionship. Since this new home was some way from work I would have to obtain a bike (no word of WLA-owned bikes reached us) and this presented two problems. The first was a lack of money to buy a mount even if one had been available (don't you know there's a war on?) and the second was an inability to ride. This second was hooted down immediately (I suspect the others were as anxious to see the last of those paste sandwiches as I was) and the first was solved by Jo who 'came across' a rusted bike in a shed. Would I give her 10/- for it? The bargain was struck and I was able to pack up my belongings and move. My new landlady was superb—she would watch for my homecoming by waiting at the window to see me sail past perched high on the squeaky bike. Then she put the kettle on and by the time the tea was brewed I had cycled to the end of the road, fallen off into the ditch, and walked back pushing that bike.

However, without a congenial family atmosphere it could be a lonely life as

Diana Powell comments:

'One thing I missed was companionship with other girls. I lived in a cottage with
two elderly ladies and all the other girls lived in the village.'

Joyce Whiteley too, with her friends Joan and Alice, was billeted with an elderly
lady:

'...who could hardly cope with the appetites we acquired after a day working in
the open air. All day we managed on a couple of cheese or beetroot sandwiches and
a piece of cake. We could have eaten horses had they been offered—I do not think
they were—for some reason I can only remember the rice puddings. Joan and I
shared a double bed and many a good laugh.

There was no bathroom and no hot water to wash in except on Saturdays. On that
day we were allowed a pint mug each of hot water for our all-over washes before
we dressed up ready to go to the Corn Exchange for the dance. After a week of
physically hard work we needed every drop of that water!'

From elderly ladies trying to cope with ravenous appetites on wartime rations to
Cold Comfort Farm and Mabel Potter who:

'...had to wash outside at the pump, it was a rough family of four sons and their
old mother. We sat at a great wooden table and she used to slice the pan loaf against
her bosom and sling it down the table to each of us. The bed was full of fleas and
when we complained to our district representative the old lady said we had brought
them with us!'

Amy Johnstone shows a glimpse of the other side of the coin—if country life was
strange to us, we were certainly strange to our landladies:

'Well, I arrived at the farm, nothing special—the farmer and his wife looked
me up and down—the make-up, the nail varnish and the curls—no wonder the
farmer's wife never liked me! She hoped I was strong enough! Aye, I needed to be.
There were two men and a boy, another young land girl and a girl (not very bright)
who helped the farmer's wife, but gone was any privacy for we three girls shared a
room so I had another weep.'

Ruby Jones had several lodgings, some good and some very bad:

'As food was rationed then, my friend and I always made friends with all the
different cooks that were stationed at Merly near the gardens. The American cooks

would bring us in lovely turkey sandwiches and doughnuts (what a change from black pudding!). They would also leave tins of fruit, oranges and other things under a tree for us. We cycled back to our lodgings with things stuffed up our jumpers and hid everything from the prying eyes of our landlady.'

Vera Campbell reminds us that Scottish WLA girls particularly were often on isolated farms, very primitive, especially for city girls, and recalls the bathing arrangements where there was no running water:

'Water is carried (after being pumped into pails) and put in the hens' pots (normally used for boiling scraps for poultry and the pig). Fill an old zinc bath with a couple of pails of cold water and light a fire under the large hens' pot. Wash top half of body—dry—put on warm jersey and try to sit in the bath for the bottom half of body. Pretty grim in cold weather.'

One of the difficulties faced by girls in private billets was loneliness. There were no other girls on the farm where Audrey Bruton worked:

'It was an isolated village with an occasional bus. The people I lived with didn't have a wireless and used to check their clocks by the bus. I was glad to move on to Martlesham and was taken to my billet with a Mr and Mrs Brett... I was still the only girl on the farm and Mr and Mrs B treated me like one of the family. They lived in a farm cottage with a shed wash house, lav outside, a pump in the garden, no electricity. Jug and basin of cold water in the bedroom and a candle for light. I had to be up at 5 a.m. and Mrs B used to leave a saucepan with cold tea from the day before and I would heat it up on the primus stove to drink before I went, also Marmite sandwiches to eat... On Sunday mornings I had one kettle of hot water and a small zinc bath which I took up to my bedroom. I used to kneel on the floor and wash my face and the top part of myself, then sit in the bath with my feet on the floor then finally stand in it to wash my feet and legs.'

Kathleen McManus found wartime menus strange:

'The first evening we had porridge with ketchup for supper. I was so hungry down it went, without the ketchup. I came from a meat and potatoes type family. Porridge was for breakfast. Don't know why I remember it so clearly.'

It may be thought that the questions of food loomed large in our thoughts—well, it would, wouldn't it? Hard work and the open air brought us enormous appetites, and sometimes when doing those boring jobs like hoeing turnips or picking potatoes we would talk of food, planning meals for the future and remembering past delights. For instance, the treat prepared for Norah Welburn has stayed in her mind all these years:

'I had some wonderful meals on that farm. I never had to take sandwiches. But one day the farmer's wife asked me if I liked bananas to which I said, "Yes, it used to be my favourite fruit." Whereupon she put one in front of me. "Do you want some cream and sugar?" she asked. "No, thank you," I said, "Just butter me some of your own home baked bread." I've never enjoyed anything as much as I did that banana.'

Betty Cutts still recalls when her employer:

'...cooked a pie and afterwards she said, "Do you know what that was?" "No," I said. She then said, "it was rook pie." How I did not bring it up I do not know... the rooks of course were from the farm.'

Later, when Betty was working with the Forestry Commission she says:

'1 cannot remember ever having anything else there but beetroot sandwiches. We were allowed 12 ozs of cheese a week. I don't know where ours went to on this job, I sure did not see mine.'

Moving on to another farm, Betty

'...was billeted in the farm attic room. The owner of the farm was in the navy with much gold braid. The foreman was running the farm and the owner's wife was in the farmhouse with her mother who was a nutcase and used to chase me round the kitchen table. In my room at night I used to wedge a chair under the door handle in case she tried to get in.'

The houses some of the girls lived in have stayed in mind and May Readey describes the one she knew:

'The farmhouse had 27 rooms. The kitchen where we lived had a table in it that was 15 feet long and also a built-in seat the same length. There were huge oak cupboards reaching almost the the ceiling. All this furniture belonged to the owner of the estate and she lived at the newer Hall. There was an oven in the back kitchen, when it was in use a fire had to be lit inside, the ashes then had to be scraped out and the food was then baked on the red hot floor of this oven. Needless to say it was never used. One of the rooms I liked best had panelled doors and a fireplace of Egyptian carving, it was quite beautiful.'

Marjorie Short, too, lived in an olde worlde cottage but there the resemblance ends:

'I was billeted with a retired carter and his wife and daughter who lived in a 16th-century cottage with stone floors, paraffin lamps and a kitchen range to cook on. The toilet was unique! It was down the garden in a shed and consisted of a long seat with three holes in it, one large, one medium and one small which had two steps up to it. Underneath it ran a stream which disappeared underground.'

To be nearer the farm where she worked, Win Wild left the hostel:

'...lodged with a conscientious objector who had come to work on the farm and to live in an old farm cottage on a hillside; it was infested with mice and had a WC in the back garden, drinking water had to be fetched from a pump down the hill and across the road. Sanitary conditions were revolting owing to the said CO having a chronic stomach complaint. We bathed once a week in the farmhouse. It took us some time to nervously tell the boss who interrupted our tale of woe, "Don't tell me any more I'll get you somewhere else." We were soon lodging in a new agricultural cottage with a young couple and two small children and next door to our elderly cowman and his two sons. Father couldn't ride a bicycle and was taken to work on the back of a tandem at 6 a.m. After an illness it was decided he should not start work until 8 a.m. and the task of taking him fell to me; a good job there was very little traffic.'

When Theo Rice joined the WLA she was able to join her cousin Bette and says:

'The bungalow Bette and I rented was modern for the time, but cooking had to be done by interoven or over the open fire. It had its own well for water, no electricity of course—we spent a small fortune on oil lamps and candles. We were both hopeless cooks but survived. One winter we expected the village carol-singers and decided to treat them to a cup of coffee. Neither of us had a clue, not having made coffee before, but we asked around and heard that salt added to the flavour. Much discussion on our part on the evening concerned as to how much salt. Eventually we decided a dessert-spoon would be sufficient. The carol singers must have gone on a pub-crawl afterwards. My mother was appalled when I told her. Bette left to work in Devon, and at Tappington Hall I lived-in with the farmer, his parents, wife and six children. I shared a bedroom with the eldest girl aged about 15 years. Fortunately there was a bathroom and hot water, but no electricity and so we had to use candles after dark. Meals were an eye-opener and I was at first inwardly horrified to eat soup through to dessert with the same utensil—a spoon. The farmer, a Scotsman, liked his porridge thick with salt. Ugh! I hated porridge with salt! Naturally sugar was rationed. And then thick slices of belly pork. My stomach revolted at first and I said goodbye to breakfast behind the cowshed, but soon I was eating both just to keep out the cold.'

Margaret Bodman has succinct comments about her various lodgings:

'Very modern farm, kind farmer and his wife, even gave me a birthday present of a hankie when I had been there only two weeks (on coupon too!). Had baths in the farmhouse. Enjoyed several Christmas dinners with my boss and family in the farmhouse, he then sent out a crate of beer for the men... Had several billets, cold, tired and hungry, worried and fed up. Was with my landlady when she received the telegram with the dreadful news that her son had been killed in the war.'

Betty Venn's landlady, Mrs Goode, was a pleasant person with one daughter:

'I fitted in well, her husband was chauffeur/ handyman to the Manor House, we lived in a smaller house called Abbots Leigh. She was a great cook and looked after me well, a little narrow-minded. Her husband, Will, had a great sense of humour. I was there three years and accepted as one of the family.'

Food continued to occupy our thoughts and those of Cynthia Banbury:

'Tea was offered twice during the long day, we scoffed our sandwiches probably by mid-morning and often waylaid an unwary baker's van to beg for stale cakes etc. I do remember very vividly being eternally hungry. The farmers were not obliged to feed us of course, but an occasional bowl of soup came our way, to be fair. Farmers were rationed as we were. Still we existed.'

In D. Heppell's case good food and company helped:

'Our first job for a fortnight was chopping thistles down, waist high. We were lucky it was lovely weather and the farmer's wife was a good cook. She kept us well fed and was good company and a good friend to us both... Then I was moved and billeted with an elderly couple in the village. Marvellous people, I was made to feel at home.'

Still on the subject of food, Olwen Owen has a grim tale.

I had said at interview that I would be happy to work in Wales as I had a fair knowledge of the language... The rather gruff farmer who met me asked at once if I spoke Welsh. Rather shy, I replied, "A little." "Right—there is no English spoken on the farm." I had an aunt living a couple of miles from the farm who became rather alarmed when she heard me speaking rather "rough" Welsh! I soon discovered that the farmer and his wife hardly spoke to each other—I was often requested to "Tell him..." or "Tell her..." My main complaint was food—or the lack of it. The farmer would thump on my bedroom door at about 5.30 a.m. He would have made a pot of tea by the time I got downstairs but this was all we had until we had finished milking 20-plus cows, by hand of course. I was "taught" by being handed a bucket and told to get on with it! When we came in several hours later it would be to a heap of sliced bread and margarine. Later, if I had found time to make butter we would have butter as a change from margarine—so our "breakfast" consisted of just that and more tea. Later, at lunch time there would be a bowl of potatoes often nothing else! Sometimes there would be vegetables if they were available in the garden— very rarely meat.

Tea time would be the repeat of breakfast—occasionally jam would appear... The only day I recall "real food" being served was when the threshing machine arrived and neighbouring farmers came to help. I was fortunate in being able to cycle to my aunt's home where she always found something for me to eat!

Eventually I asked the WLA representative if I could live with my aunt where I would be fed! The representative visited the farm to the fury of the farmer who flatly refused to allow me to "live out". I later heard that the representative was anxious to remain on good terms with the farmer who supplied her with such rarities as eggs and cream! We very rarely had eggs on the menu. The farmer had a bad reputation as an employer and I heard many tales about former employees who had left—I did not have the option, of course.

Then one day I jammed my hand in a rusty iron gate. Blood poisoning developed and I went home on sick leave. I went to my local GP who asked at once if I was getting enough to eat. He wrote to the Land Army and told them he would not sign me as being fit to work until they found me somewhere I would be fed properly... I often think of the bleak, comfortless kitchen of that first farm. Only a wooden settle and a few wooden chairs for seating. One large scrubbed wooden table and one small circular table. During the long dark evenings the oil lamp sat on this table and the farmer wrapped his copy of *The Farmer and Stockbreeder* round the lamp preventing anybody else from reading... I think many of us owe a debt of gratitude to the then WVS who ran canteens in Menai Bridge and Bangor. It was such a joy to get a short time away from the farm and enjoy the luxury of beans on toast etc... My sparsely furnished bedroom had a hard straw mattress and I soon found that I could actually lie on the bolster which was softer! ...After I left I heard that the farmer had been deprived of his right to farm by the War Agricultural Committee. I often wonder at the lack of caring and welfare conditions generally in the Land Army. The services had all sorts of provisions for sorting out problems. Factories (at a time when many girls were drafted into munitions factories) were well served by trades unions. We seemed to be helpless in some very unpleasant situations. Perhaps it was our isolation which made life difficult in some way—and prevented organised revolt!'

On contacting the WVS about their role during the war in looking after land girls they tell me it mainly consisted of providing hot pies and layettes where necessary.

Julia Porteous had her memoirs published in a local newspaper as well as being in the Imperial War Museum:

'Miss Crawford took me to Skemrigg Farm and we met Mrs Wharrie, the farmer's wife, and I was taken into the house. Mrs Wharrie showed me to my bedroom and my first reaction was—no electricity! However, the room was nice and comfortable and I soon got used to the paraffin lamps... I put on my overalls and milking coat and boots and went to feed the hens, which was to be one of my jobs in future. It was then time to go to the byre, as it was a dairy farm... They did not have any family and I was soon to be treated as a daughter. My parents visited and stayed on occasions also. Mr Wharrie told me a few weeks later that he said to his wife, "That wee white-faced lassie will never be fit for work here," but he soon changed his mind... The food on the farm was entirely different from our small rations in the town. We churned our own butter, killed our own pig and had plenty of eggs, and occasionally they would shoot a pheasant or two so we ate very well.'

Some girls lived and looked after themselves in caravans, farm cottages or bungalows and Phyllis Munn tells of her home in a rather stark caravan:

'The caravan which was to be our home for the next year bore no resemblance to the luxurious models seen today, and it had none of the conveniences accepted as normal in a modern caravan... There were four of us and our basic needs appeared to have been catered for fairly adequately until it struck us that no provision had been made for one essential natural function. Light finally dawned as we grasped the significance of the large number of galvanised buckets with which we had been so generously supplied—it was clear these were not all intended to be used for collecting drinking and washing water... We became friendly with the wife of a farmer who kindly allowed us the daily use of her bathroom, with the added bonus of a weekly soak in a hot bath.'

Agnes Aspinall was one of a foursome in a cottage:

'I went into a cottage on a farm called Shellacres. I shared with another three girls, we got on so well together. We took turns with the cooking and cleaning. While working at Shellacres I injured my middle finger of my right hand. I caught my fingers in the cogs of a potato riddle... I left Shellacres sadly after one of my friends died of TB—she shared the cottage with us.'

Violet Farrant and those in the house with her were well looked after:

'My first farm was at Overbury near Bredon. It was a large estate owned by the Holland Martings. It was in a lovely village. We lived in a nice house, there were about eight of us and a housekeeper provided by our employer... We were allowed to go to Overbury Court, our employer's home, and get books from a very good library.'

Caroline Blyth also was one of a foursome:

'I transferred to Armisfield Mains Farm and was 20 miles from Edinburgh, near Haddington. At the farm there were another three land girls and we lived together in one of the farm cottages. Each week in turn we had mornings off to do our housework and the cooking and shopping. This worked out very well and it was a pleasant two mile walk to the shops.'

Pat Detrey was, with two others, in a farm cottage:

'...Our cottage was pretty primitive—no bathroom, and only a cold water tap in the kitchen. Primus stoves to boil our kettles and an old black range in the living room, which we cooked on. Our loo was the little house at the end of the garden. I was gardener-in-chief and we grew all our own vegetables—had gallons of milk of course and the cracked eggs from the farmer's wife. Harvest rations were extra cheese and margarine.

We used to make ourselves lovely "cheese dreams" for breakfast—after three hours work milking we were more than ready for them. Another thing I learned was to cook, as we took it in turns to make our main meal. Not for us, after a hard day's work to go home to a ready cooked meal as the farm men did, we had to set to and get it ourselves.'

After about 18 months in a hostel Mabel Williams and her friend went into private digs and worked at one particular farm:

'Our digs were in the house of the gamekeeper. It was a very old house. His wife cooked on a kitchen range and a paraffin stove was placed on the table at breakfast time, on which we cooked bacon and toasted bread. We had no electricity and only candlelight to go to bed. There was a paraffin lamp on the table during the dark evenings. There was no running water, only a pump at the sink. There was an outside toilet down the garden—no flush but ashes to cover whatever!

As for a bath, this was not possible very often. It was a tin bath, put in the kitchen, and water had to be heated in pails on the kitchen range. My friend and I shared the same water and even that wasn't very hot!'

Joan Welbourn also transferred, with her friend Joan Allen, to Llanfair Caereinion:

'...we were put into a private house, the Misses Williams. We shared a huge double bed—pictures everywhere of Lloyd George, tiny house by the river. Joan was always helpful, always chopped the sticks.'

Nancy Johnson evidently made friends for life in her billet:

'I was billeted with an insurance agent, his wife and four daughters, the eldest eleven years, the youngest 18 months. The whole family was extremely good to me and I was with them for ten years, staying on after the WLA was abolished. The parents passed away but I am still in touch with the four daughters.'

Again, it's the basics that remain in the memory as Sylvia Dean Cawley says:

'Then the farmer found me private digs with one of our farm workers. A nice clean home. But she only had tinned milk and I had to buy fresh. And the toilet was down the garden. We didn't have one on the farm for workers but to see it now, it's all mod cons with everything you can think of.'

Joy Eichler has a different story:

'My boss and his wife were titled people with four children—all younger than me. They were very good to me and I lived in the farmhouse and was treated as one of the family. It can't have been easy having an 18-year-old addition and must have been a worry when I sometimes stayed out late, going to the pictures with WLA friends and having to bike back 2½ miles in the dark.'

Enid Ballard and her friend were billeted in the pub:

'The good food we had in The Bull made other girls envious. Mr Goodings used to shoot peasant and deer etc. but sometimes it was 9 p.m. before we had it. Only had two rounds of sandwiches, a piece of cake and an apple from 7 a.m. My friend had an ulcer.'

Jean Barnes tells of her first posting—that should never have been:

'At the end of the month the farmer should have started paying me. When the cash I had taken with me had gone I drew out of my post office book money to pay for my lodgings at the gamekeeper's home where I was staying. After ten weeks I wrote to the Land Army and they sent the local lady who was appointed to watch over WLA girls. She arrived (on horseback) and I said I would like a transfer as I was not being paid. She agreed and then went to speak to the farmer who came out in a tearing rage saying; "I hear you are hard up." I left and was sent to another farm.'

Mary Becraft found the funny side:

'My first shock came when May and I had gone to a village dance. Mrs Osborne said she would leave supper for us. The supper was one bottle of light ale, one hunk of bread and about ¼lb of cheese, plus pickles! As a young lady who had been brought up to eat thin bread and butter I was undecided how to start, but I learned very quickly and enjoyed my suppers very much! ...Bath night was hilarious. We used to light a fire under an old stone copper out in a shed—fill up same with rain water. We put the tin bath in front of the kitchen range—then it was a bucket chain from shed to kitchen. We had to be quick!'

Lilian Gerber, now living at Niagara Falls, tells us:

'The landlady had said I would have to leave as I ate too much. A pint of pudding did her and her husband two days before I went there, she had no children, also it was extra for a bath and extra for washing. I was expected to wash by candlelight and use only a quart jug of water.'

And Win Wild brings our stories of private billets to a clerical ending:

'Our first billet was in part of the rectory at Stanton-by-Bridge near Derby. Until our bicycles arrived we had a lift to work in the Rector's car. He would greet us in the morning with, "Don't forget your provender," and as we drove down a gated road would say, "Ah rejoice the gate is already open."'

Those who were sent to hostels had the advantage of companionship with other girls, were looked after by a warden, and were allocated work by a forewoman. Enid Bennell paints a vivid picture:

'Leaving home, that was when the butterflies started, we had to all meet at a station a lorry met us and took us to our hostel which was a few miles from town. The hostel was up a tree-lined drive with meadows each side. It was a beautiful house, it was called Larkstone and I thought it was a lovely name to go with the surroundings. Our warden was a delightful lady—I don't know how she managed to keep us all in order but she did... We slept so many to a room, it was strange sleeping and living with a crowd of girls. I think I was the youngest. The first one in at night got in the bathroom first.'

Betty Schibler remembers the hostel was situated up a long and steep hill and

'...the night going back up the hill when it was dark and very foggy I could hear footsteps quite loudly. There was nowhere to run so I went close to the hedge scared with fright. A white form appeared out of the fog and then I realised it was a solitary white cow making its way down the hill. At the top was the hostel originally built for POWs. A lovely welcome from 20 WLAs, fun and laughter all day long even when we were working hard. We returned at night after five and how we used to enjoy the evening meal, usually a roast with crispy potatoes, followed usually by spicy and hot bread pudding and mugs of tea.'

The other side of the hostel coin from Sylvia Dean Cawley:

'I was in a servants' annexe of a large house four miles away from the farm. There was no covering on the wooden flooring. In our room two bunks and a single bed, two chairs and a hurricane lamp for light. There were about 20 of us in this hostel... In the morning I queued up for breakfast which consisted of bread, one rasher of bacon and half a tomato, which I stuck between the bread and ate on the cycle ride to work. In winter it was dark and starlit and very cold. Our food in general was bad, and the extra cheese we were allowed, rotten with mould. One day it upset one girl as we sat in the orchard eating and we decided enough was enough and we asked our farmer if we could take our complaint to head office in Canterbury. He asked to see what we had for lunch, which was a piece of bread and stale cheese and two slices of cucumber. And he and his kind wife fed us with milk and food for several days, while he went to Canterbury on our behalf saying it was disgusting... The outcome was that the hostel was watched at weekends and it was found that our cooks were caught taking away large suitcases full of our food to their homes or black market. We were found a replacement and things improved, but could have been better.'

Elsie Druce was leaving home for the first time, home being Newbiggin-by-Sea, a fishing village dominated all round by coal mines:

'...a truck took us to Bamburgh and our hostel, a lovely house which had been requisitioned for the job. It had three large bedrooms with three double bunks in each, one spare bedroom for visitors and our warden's room. We met our warden, all five foot one of her. She called us her children and became our champion when it came to getting our rations in the village, especially from the butcher. The village ladies shopping in the same shop as our Miss Walch would question our extra agricultural meat ration but this tiny lady, 71 years old, brought out of retirement to do so, knew all the answers to those ladies. She made rules for us like being in by 9.30, we needed the sleep she said. But she never knew about the drain pipes (or did she?).

Our cook was chosen from the village, another unmarried elderly lady who looked after her mother. She loved being with us girls, her life had been quiet up till then. Some evenings we would do the washing up for her so enabling her to go home earlier to her mother. On wet days that were too wet the farmers rang up for us not to turn up. On these days we cleaned the hostel, helped the cook. I always got the job of chopping the wood for the stove as I seemed to have the patience. Nellie (the cook) said to do them nice and small.'

Ann Bibbings had memories of a gruesome incident:

'One evening the army had been on exercises and were returning back to their lorry, walking up the road in ones and twos by our hostel. A couple of the boys had a hand grenade and decided they would let it off in the driveway of our hostel. Well, something went wrong and before they could throw it, it went off and one of the boys lost his arm and the other an eye. We didn't get much sleep that night.'

Joan Welbourn's first hostel sounds a shocker:

'We were met at the railway station, Welshpool, and taken in a truck to Llwydiath. The hostel had been for Italian POWs—you didn't travel to work, you were already there. I think I cried for a week. The food was terrible, gravy was cabbage water. Peanut butter and Marmite sandwiches. Our work was chopping bracken down, clearing the land for the cattle to graze... by Saturday all the land girls were moved from this hostel into Welshpool as it was said that the hostel was not suitable for girls. We moved to Severn House, ATS girls used to be housed there—lovely fires and really go upstairs to bed. Eight girls to a room with a wardrobe and dressing table each and electric light.'

Gladys Benton worked on a large farm:

'...so most of us had broken down bicycles to get from field to field. After a hard day's work, we would ride back to the hostel and scramble for the bathrooms, since there were only two between the 40 of us. We would then have dinner. Unfortunately the food was not very good, but we survived.'

Mabel Williams also has recollections of food—or its absence:

'Each girl was given a pack of sandwiches. If you were lucky you had a tin lunchbox in which to put them, otherwise you rolled up the sandwiches in newspaper, hoping that they would remain reasonably fresh for lunchtime. The warden gave each gang a small quantity of tea and sugar, or cocoa and sugar, hoping that the farmer's wife would make us a jug of hot tea or cocoa for lunch time. At some farms we went to they refused to do so, and all we had to drink was water if we could find any... Some of the farmers who refused to make us a drink had their names crossed off our work-sheets which were kept in the office at the hostel. We didn't go back to those farms again. After a few months some farmers would phone in to the hostel for a certain gang to go back to the farm, and some farmers' wives were very kind to us. Tea and food were rationed, but they would bake a large tray of potatoes for us. This was really appreciated. During harvest time it was a long day, and there was very little to eat, sandwiches for lunch and sandwiches for tea! Food and sweets were rationed.

When the work was done and we returned to the hostel our dinner would be waiting for us, often lukewarm. Sometimes it had been kept warm for one to two hours and the warden did her best. But when you are hungry you eat most things, and even a slice of dry bread helps to fill you up.'

Dorothy Coonrod, who now lives in Florida, worked for three years on a farm at Handley Castle near Upton-on-Severn.

'Lady Lechmere from Handley Castle took care of our welfare, about ten girls, and invited us to her beautiful home, gave garden parties for us, and she had all the flowers cut and placed in the church for my wedding.'

Jean Doe found the work was tough but loved the hostel life:

'At the hostel the warden was a Mrs Drake-Brockman and her assistant Irene Howell—we were disciplined but got a lot of fun trying to break the rules. Mrs Drake-Brockman would organise everyone in a play which we would then take round to the village halls—all this after a day's work! Winter and summer alike. The money raised went, I believe, to the WLA Benevolent Fund.'

Dorothy Fox was posted to Glyn Hall Hostel at Pontypool:

'They couldn't have sent me much further from home and I was delighted, just to get away from my father, who was something of a tyrant. When I arrived at Glyn Hall I found that it was a munitions factory hostel and not a large old house as I'd expected... Four more girls from Yorkshire travelled to the same hostel and two others only stayed a week and thought that the work was too hard, so they packed up and went home...

The hostel consisted of hutments where two girls shared a bedroom with hand basins, toilets and bathrooms were at the end of each block and there were communal dining rooms, writing rooms and lounges... We got some jolly good meals at some of the farms and then had a dinner to go back to at the hostel. The hostel dinners were good but we were expected to put sweet pickle, cheese and piccalilli into sandwiches. I've never liked piccalilli since, I can see the stuff oozing through the bread and the edges curled up because it was such hot weather—ugh!

In January 1945 we had a heavy snowfall, which prevented us from getting to work for almost a week, and as it didn't appear to be clearing we were given permission to go home. We had to walk the five miles into Abergavenny, dragging our luggage on home-made sledges! The 5 p.m. from Abergavenny to Crewe arrived at 9.30 p.m. and I had to sit on a sailor's knee most of the way—a great hardship! I eventually arrived home at 5.45 a.m. One of the problems that beset us was keeping our hair clean especially while working in amongst straw and hay, and we discovered to our horror and dismay after feeling itchy for a few days that one of our number was "lousy" literally. So we had a massive clean up of heads with Derbac. I had my hair cut short after that so that it was easier to keep clean.

Barbara Wickenden, fruit farming in Essex, did not lack company:

'About 20 girls lived in a farmhouse as a hostel, with staff of a cook and housekeeper. We kept our own bedroom clean, sleeping six to a room in double bunks. Food was neither good nor plentiful; most of us were able to supplement from home and of course we ate pounds of apples. We were up at 5.15 a.m. reporting for instructions for the day's work... We went back for a porridge breakfast and to make sandwiches for our lunch, eaten in the working place. These could be mostly bread and marg plus spam or anything we brought from home visits... We came back to the hostel at 5.30 p.m. usually to wash and have a cooked meal. There was one bathroom, two loos—no showers of course nor wash bowls in the bedrooms. How did we cope? Loos in the field were trenches surrounded by sacking for privacy. I spied a stoat once just below me – I hopped up very quickly. We were not very warm in winter as there was no central heating and there was quite a deal of crying over homesickness, partings and romances.'

Joan Williams was sent to St Mary's in the Marsh, a WLA hostel in Kent:

'We met four other girls there who were to become part of our gang of 13 girls who worked on a seed farm on the Romney Marsh...

Our first sight of the hostel made us wonder what we had let ourselves in for as it seemed so isolated after living in London, but it was so peaceful.

There were about 60 girls living in the hostel a very happy, friendly crowd... There were two bunk beds in each cubicle, and my one vivid memory is the fight to get a Tilley lamp each evening for our cubicle as there never seemed to be enough in working order to go round, it was always a fight to get a bath as there were only three bathrooms and the first there got the hot water, if you were last it was luke warm or cold. Washing our clothes was another problem too as all wearing the same type of uniform even though we marked them with our names sometimes things would disappear from the drying room... There is one other thing that I shall never forget—the packed lunches we were given to keep us going in the fields, always a piece of dry fruit cake, and bloater paste sandwiches which made us so thirsty. I've worked in a food shop since leaving the WLA and bloater paste always brings back that memory.'

Ivy Walker, another Yorkshire girl, seems to have enlivened life in her hostel:

'Our cook at the hostel was Scottish and our hearts (three Yorkshire girls) would sink when she told us she had a treat for us – Yorkshire pudding. I think she was in league with the local dentist on a commission basis as the puddings were like leather! I always seemed to be in bother, like the time I auctioned the new warden's goods and chattels by mistake, or when I took a goose home and the blood dripped through the sack from the luggage rack onto a young sailor who gave me a look of horror and fled up the corridor...

Getting home for us Yorkshire girls was a feat of endurance. We got the bus to Didcot, train to Oxforrd, change to Sheffield train, spend the night on Sheffield station as we were not allowed into the NAAFI, then get the milk train to Penistone, then to Huddersfield and lastly a bus to Mirfield.'

Marjorie Rossi was housed in a derelict reconditioned farmhouse:

'The farmhouse had no bathroom, it had a bath which we had to boil water for, no inside loo, it was an Elsan in a hut outside. Our housekeeper was a not very pleasant lady. Our first meal after travelling all day was two sausages and mashed

potatoes, we were starving... Our meals were pathetic, for the first five days there
was nothing but Marmite and bread for our sandwiches and only two slices, our
meal on our return was again sausages and mash for the whole week, later on we
progressed to cheese and the odd egg.'

Joan Shakesheff found that time helped to overcome homesickness and
acclimatise one to a new life and attendant problems:

'As time passed and overcoming homesickness too, things became easier, now
living in a hostel with 40 other land girls, which was a lovely old rectory house,
where water and electricity were pumped by generator in the grounds. Bath water
limited to one bath a week (three inches of water remember). It brought problems
with so many of us arriving back very dirty. Often the generator failed to pump,
cutting off the electricity supply too. At these times storm lanterns were placed
on each landing for light. We used to tell the new recruits, known as "rookies",
that the house was haunted. Proceeding to scare them with creaking doors and
things that went bump in the night. Sometimes returning to your bunk bed from
the bathroom you found it had become an apple pie bed, and took ages to find
your way in, if at all. One girl returned to find a dried sheep's head in hers. We
heard her screams, in the dark, from the top floor, and it gave us all a laugh.'

The girls were prepared to work hard but injustice or unfairness was not to be
tolerated, as Joan Turner says:

'The Matron was an old battleaxe. Christmas time we used to have things given
to us from the village and the brewer gave us wine and sherry but she never told us
about it, she would keep it for herself. But we fixed her. One of the girls knew where
she kept her bottle of gin and she emptied half of it out and filled it up with water...
she said someone had been in her room but we never said a word.'

Ivy Mooney was stationed at Lakenheath in Suffolk:

'The hostel was just outside the village. There were about six large sleeping
quarters and a separate dining room. We didn't lack entertainment. We had regular
invitations to Lakenheath Air Base to dances and the Army would send trucks from
Wildenhall, Thetford and Brandon to entertain us.'

Looking back Joy Morgan sees as fun her experiences:

'...an old rectory in St Columb Major which was very well haunted and many
strange things happened. Our boyfriends were very nervous coming to pick us up.'

Connie McNichol's hostel may not have been haunted but the erstwhile owner must have experienced a frisson or two:

'In July 1942 along with six other girls from Glasgow of very varying social backgrounds, shapes and sizes. I found myself installed in the Abbey Arms Hotel in the beautiful village of New Abbey. The top floor of the old and dingy hotel had presumably been requisitioned to form the first Land Army hostel in the area and naturally the elderly owner was not at all pleased to have us. She kept a 10-inch blade meat cleaver behind the side door to the building which we had to use and we were all firmly convinced that at least one of us would be found one day chopped to pieces.

We were told by our local Welfare Representative, Mrs John McMyn of Kirkhouse, Kirkbean, a farmer's wife, that we would each work at a different farm every week wherever extra help was needed; that our duties would be telephoned to us each Sunday evening; and that our pay would be sent from the office in Castle Douglas. One girl would be "on cook" each week and had to do the shopping, cleaning etc for seven people! No thought had been given as to how we were to exist until the first pay day at the end of the next week, so, as well as being the first housekeeper/cook I had to subsidise the six others by paying for all the food bought, as no one else had more than a few shillings... I sallied forth to the village shop on the Monday morning with a long list... but without our ration books which had to be sent off to Kirkcudbright for presumably change of address, there was little or nothing available. A frantic telephone call to Mrs McMyn brought forth some help, and the information that on market day she and her husband would take the "cook" into Dumfries to do the shopping. How these people could have expected one girl to make beds, wash dishes, clean, and cook for six other people, total strangers, and herself, I cannot fathom, but I certainly know that I was never more tired than at the end of that first week in the Land Army. Working in the fields was a cake-walk after that!'

Forty seems to have been the usual number of occupants for most hostels as Joan Hawell records:

'The train from Paddington to Oxford that morning was buzzing with WLA girls in stiff new breeches and heavy brown shoes which needed special guidance. In fact there were 37 girls in all heading for Woodstock Hostel. Friendships were established on that train that lasted many years and fears were calmed. The hostel was equipped to house 40 girls. Besides the 37 of us there were three Nottingham girls. These three seemed to have had some previous WLA experience. We all lived very happily together and shared most things, even our clothes... A normal day started with a call at 6.30 a.m. breakfast at 7. We collected our sandwiches, which had been cut ready for us, placed them in our WLA issued lunch tins together with a flask of tea and were ready for our journey to work. It was approximately 6 p.m. when we arrived back at base. There was a grand scuffle for a bath, with dinner at 7 p.m.'

Daphne Jauncey was sent to a hostel in Horsell (Woking), called the Old Rectory:

'...as I remember not far from the Red Lion – here I learnt to drink whisky and orange, I never really liked it! Most of the other girls came from the London area, and were a mixed bunch to say the least, oh the swear words I learnt. I had always led a sheltered life. We had lots of fun though. The food was horrible, so I was lucky that I could get home quite often for a feed. I can remember slightly mouldy bread for our sandwiches, which we all did ourselves every morning. We ate raw potatoes, swedes, turnips, anything we could get, we were always hungry.'

Hilary Lawn was at Wheatsheaf House in East Ilsley, near Newbury:

'The Wheatsheaf hostel had only ten land girls being the smallest in Berkshire. East Ilsley was quite a small village and only two houses had piped water at that time, the rest having wells. The electricity came through overhead cables and just a small amount of snow used to bring them down leaving us without power... Soon after I left the hostel a lorry crashed into the front of Wheatsheaf House and damaged it badly. All the girls had to leave as they decided to close it down.'

During the last six months of her Land Army time Joanna Murray was in a hostel with improved conditions:

'...doing relief milking or working with the gang, but working eight hours or so a day instead of dawn till dark, and having running water and electricity, being able to bath and do washing and being well fed.'

So many girls seemed to miss out on these basics. Elizabeth Anderson, in the Timber Corps, gives her picture:

'In my first camp near Kelso in the Scottish borders there were over 30 of us. We were 12 to a sleeping hut, and there was a dining hut, an ablutions hut and another for leisure hours, which contained an old piano and we had singsongs etc.
The huts were heated by a log-burning stove and we took turns at sawing the logs to keep them burning during the evenings. They were all lit by paraffin lamps—very primitive! In the wintertime if one was lucky enough to own a hot water bottle it was

usually frozen by the morning. When we were up in the woods our lunch was sent up by tractor. It was usually just sandwiches but one day each week we got a hot pie. There was always a huge urn of boiling hot tea which was really relished by the girls.'

Joan Wright had to report to the Wateringbury hostel on New Year's Eve which she thought was a bit much:

'We had a matron over us and had to be in by a certain time or the door was locked. We packed our sandwiches for the day while eating breakfast and then were taken by lorry to our place of work. Anyone working a short distance away could use the WLA bikes, which I might add were nearly dropping to bits.'

Betty Otway was at Usk, Monmouthshire Agricultural Institute which was normally for agricultural students, but for the duration of the war and until the disbanding of the WLA it was used as a hostel for the Land Army:

'Out of the original 60 I can only remember two girls opting out after the first two weeks, not being conscripts this was possible I suppose. Our arrival must have been quite a shock to the local people, I guess, in that beautiful and very quiet corner of Monmouthshire. However, once they got used to seeing us about and realised that girls from large towns were really fairly harmless, if somewhat noisy at times at local hops etc. in competition with the village girls for the attention of the young Romeos of the area, which after all just added a bit of gossip and was fun to watch I should imagine. As for us, it was comical to hear the different accents and turns of speech when we spoke to each other, we all needed some interpretations for a while, but considering that we all came from the same country it was a revelation. As time went on we had Welsh girls, Londoners, a few Yorkshire lasses and even a Swiss girl, joined us.'

I. Pamphlett spent 3½ years with the Land Army, all at the same place in Suffolk:

'I remember it took quite a while for the farmers to accept us... The first job we had was at a farm next to us and we had to hoe sugar beet and single it out. The trouble was we did not know the weeds from the beet, so we were hoeing the lot off. We only had Sunday off which was not a very nice day as we only had cold meat, as there was no staff; they all had the day off. We had our rest day on Saturdays, the best day of the week.

We all had to look after our own rations, which were very small. We had our own sugar, butter and marge. We also had one flask given to us but most of them got broken so we just used to take a bottle of water with our lunch. It was OK in the summer but hard on us in winter. We used to love doing hedging and ditching as we could light a fire and toast our bread on our pitchforks. Sometimes it fell off but we used to get very hungry so we did not worry about the ash on it and sometimes we could get hold of a potato and put it in the ash.'

Cynthia Banbury found life in the hostel a far cry from home comforts:

'...the first startling jolt to the system was landing in Oldberrow Rectory, used as a WLA
hostel in November 1945, completely untrained and shown the dormitory for about six
to eight girls. The sleeping arrangements were spartan to say the least, mine the top bunk,
wooden slats and about two inches of a straw-filled palliasse in place of a spring mattress.
Two rough army blankets, no sheets or pillow cases. The next day up at 6 a.m. to hastily
make two sandwiches to last the day until 6 p.m.'

Margaret Coulson-Loam, too, found life at the Forestry School at Parkend rather a
shock:

'...I had to share a dormitory with six other women of different backgrounds. I had led
a sheltered life, being "a lady of leisure" not having mixed with working class of those days
it was an experience.'

Our pay varied widely. There were standard county agricultural rates set but even so
there were differences. We should all have been paid overtime rates, particularly during
the long harvest days, but many of us were not. I once recieved a small harvest bonus
whilst working on a market garden—no two girls had the same amount and there was
no indication of how the sum was arrived at. Joan Hawell comments:

'Oxfordshire I understand was one of the better counties regarding wages. We had 48/-
for 48 hours. Each girl received 24/- in a weekly packet. 24/- was retained by HQ for
subsistence. Overtime pay was earned at the busiest times, e.g. haymaking and harvest,
when some would work until eight or nine o'clock at night.'

I. Pamphlett's figures were slightly different:

'We did a 52 hour week all for £2.4s. and out of that we paid £1.10s. board.'

Joyce Sansom produces yet other figures:

'Our wages started at 28/- and rose to 32/-, 21/- for our board and lodging left me very
little, only enough for soap and toothpaste. When the wages went up to 32/- I bought a
bicycle on the "never never". What bliss! I worked a twelve hour day and no overtime at all
but after about three years a union man appeared and insisted that I was paid overtime, it
was not much but it helped.'

So there were differences between girls serving in one part of the country and another, as well as between the WLA as a whole and others doing war work. Julia Porteous says:

'I always think the WLA was the Cinderella service as we did not get the recognition the other services got or cheap travel or demob clothes or gratuity, and we did our best for the war effort with hard work and long hours.'

Olga Tremayne comments too on the hazards of farm work:

'People used to say to me, "What a nice healthy job", but I had more things wrong with me then than in civilian life. I caught pneumonia working in the snow, dermatitis from a mangy cow. I fell from a rick and sprained an arm, and caught athlete's foot from having wet feet. I was almost dragged under an iron wheel by my raincoat and I had two encounters with bulls. One chased me up the yard and I got into the shed just in time, and the other pinned me in a corner, when luckily I had a bale of straw in my arms into which he was digging his horns. Fortunately the cowman heard me call and drove it off. Of the eight girls I trained with, half were invalided out in the first year. I was told that far more girls were invalided out of the Land Army than the other services and the numbers were kept quiet. Some girls had tractors overturning on them and were in wheelchairs.'

Time and again these letters question what we considered (and still do) to be an unfairness in our treatment as against that of the armed forces. Well, were the ATS armed? And anyway we were well and truly armed—you should have seen us with a pitchfork! Olga Tremayne goes on:

'One meanness I encountered was when I went to London on a day off in my uniform because I was eager to see the American "Stage Door Canteen" which was open to all servicemen and wornen. I was stopped by the English doorman who said, "You are not armed forces, you can't go in." I said, "I only want to stand inside to see it." He just stonily repeated, "You can't go in." How mean can you get!'

Joyce Sherman had a simliar experience:

'I recall being refused admission to the NAAFI because the WLA was not regarded as a fighting force.'

Diana Powell too, still remembers unjust treatment:

'The other thing which I thought unfair was that we didn't have the perks the other services had. I had one week off a year, no train passes... and also at the end of the week I had one shilling and sixpence left to buy everything else needed.'

Betty Campbell, too, finds, our post-war treatment inequitable:

'I have since been quite annoyed that we weren't considered as forces, and didn't qualify
for gratuities and automatic membership for certain clubs like the others. I'm sure we
made a much more useful contribution than some, and worked damned hard for our
money.'

6

TRAINING

For some, training meant a four or six week course at an agricultural college, for others time spent working on a farm counted as training before a permanent posting. Others however, went straight in at the deep end. Sympathy here both for the girls and those who employed them!

My own experience started at the Seale Hayne Agricultural College at Newton Abbot—no doubt this was the life, spring time in Devon! I had asked for market gardening and my clearest memory of that time was of a line of girls advancing across a field, each holding a dibber in one hand and a potato in the other. 'Old Jim' was our teacher and he managed to stay good humoured and smiling as we milled around, his red face beaming and his cap at an angle over one ear, saying repeatedly as he demonstrated, 'You digs a liddle pit,' then dropping a potato neatly inside it before moving on. I don't quite know what this labour intensive operation taught us, except that hours spent stooping whilst moving across an area which appeared to increase in size as we went made one very reluctant to stand upright at the end of a row, and even more reluctant to bend again at the start of the next. Only Old Jim remained beaming and tireless.

Molly Campbell, too, went to the Seale Hayne, though she trained for farm work:

'Seale Hayne College provided the embryo land girls with training in various kinds of farm work. We were divided into groups of three or four and did a different job each day. Our first day was spent in "milking" a rubber udder filled with water, before we were let loose on the long-suffering cows. That was, of course, long before the days of all farms having milking machines. Work started at 5.30 a.m. and ended at 4 p.m. On our second day we were introduced to the heavy horses and learnt to groom them before putting on their harness and going out into the fields for ploughing, harrowing, fetching marigolds and hay. It was rather an alarming experience to fetch the horses from their stalls and lead them slipping and sliding on the frosty cobbles to the trough which on that first day was covered with ice. On the third day we were introduced to the tractor and had a lesson about the engine, and shown the difficulty of starting it with paraffin. More harrowing and ploughing.

Our fourth day was delightful, working with the shepherd, Davy. He liked a "proper" job to be done, and demonstrated hedging and ditching. He was a lovely old man (I guess actually he was about 50!) and I think we all enjoyed our days with him best. Finally on the fifth day we spent the time with the pigs and poultry, the most boring, we all felt. Our month was spent on this rota. Little did we realise that life on ordinary farms would bear little resemblance to being students at an agricultural college. In my case reality would soon overtake fantasy.'

Branwen Weekes trained for gardening and is also uncertain about the usefulness of the skills acquired.

'We went to the Cannington Farm Institute in Bridgewater the following February, not an ideal time of the year to learn the mysteries of gardening. It was cold and wet and unutterably bleak for the whole month. Before breakfast we all trooped out to a freezing shed to pick weevils out of a pile of beans. Then when it grew light enough, out we went to turn over a fibre heap. Both were horrid jobs. An old man taught us how to sharpen a saw, looking down the length of its blade and bending with a special tool those teeth which weren't quite true. That and learning the morse code when I was a Girl Guide have proved to be amongst the least useful of all the skills I have acquired through the years. The only pleasant thing I can remember doing was setting out tomato plants in the warm and steamy greenhouses. Between these we planted lettuce seedlings and between these we buried old carrots. Every morning we pulled up the old carrots, cut out the wireworm and replanted them. Given the choice, wireworm love little tomato plants and they love little lettuce plants, but best of all they love old carrots. I think that was about the only useful thing I learnt during the whole dreary month.'

After about a year of market gardening I asked to be transferred to dairy work and was sent to train at Limpsfield Lodge Farm. Living and working with other girls was fun and the farm was kept spick and span as there were many willing hands to keep it so.

I remember being taught hedging and ditching and experiencing a real sense of achievement as the hedge looked so good as we moved steadily along it, the bonfires of trimmings burning alongside us to be doused by nightfall before the arrival of enemy planes. So rarely does one now see a beautiful hedge cared for in this way—I caught sight of one recently whilst driving through Hereford and was immediately taken back to those days at Limpsfield.

We were of course shown how to muck out, leaving a clean and wholesome cowshed. On my first day on the farm to which I was posted I was told to muck out and did so with gusto much to the horror of the cowman who returned from his elevenses to find that the muck of ages had been moved. This wasn't the way to do it apparently, just clear the gully and spread a bit of clean straw where neccessary. Olga Tremayne also trained at Limpsfield and remembers:

'The farm was run by a married couple, the wife cooking and running the house and the husband teaching us farm work... The regime was fairly strict, and we had to be in by 10 p.m. The food wasn't bad except that pudding was rice pudding every day with bright pink blancmange on Sunday without fail.

There were eight other girls and although the Land Army was badly treated in the way of appreciation and privileges, not even officially allowed into canteens, the *Daily Mail* gave us a gramophone with a few records, which was greatly appreciated and much used.'

Audrey Bagnall too went to Limpsfield Lodge:

'It was a bitterly cold, dark, winter's morning when we set out... we saw a house loom up through the snow, there was a long low line of buildings. We could hear cattle lowing, girls' voices and see flickering lamps... One of the first things that struck me was, there was no electricity. There were open fires, Tilley lamps and a calor gas cooker... A girl called Sylvia, who came from the Hulme area of Manchester, was in a bed near me. I could not help but wonder if she was very shy, as she got into bed wearing all her underwear and socks and then proceeded to wriggle out of her things under the bedclothes and put them under the pillow whilst I undressed and folded my things by the bed...

My watch showed 5.40 a.m. The other girls were stirring and Sylvia did a complete reversal of the previous night's routine, she emerged from under the bedclothes needing only her overalls and boots. As I shivered into my cold clothes I realised it wasn't modesty that made Sylvia undress and dress in bed, it was a warm start to face the day. Sylvia knew a thing or two! She told me to just have a wee, and not to bother with a wash until breakfast time, because you got your face chapped.

Everyone went out to the sheds, the air was as keen as a knife and took your breath away. We had to dig the snow away from the shed doors before we could get them open. The cows came lumbering in, great steaming beasts, each one knew her own stall and woe betide any cow that ventured into her neighbour's place... My first lesson in dairying was to "keep out of the way" as the cattle came past, eyes rolling and horns tossing. It was about 8 a.m. by the time we went in to breakfast, I felt I had done a day's work already and it was barely coming light. Breakfast was a time to get a proper wash and make your bed...

Later I was with the girls cleaning the sheds. The dung had to be shovelled up out of the gutters and barrowed outside. The sheds were swept and swilled clean. I think the job the girls detested, especially in that awful cold weather, was "troughing" which entailed scrubbing out each stone trough with cold water and even colder hands. My hands were so numb and cold that even though I knocked skin off my knuckles I didn't feel it, till my hands warmed up again. When the sheds were done we had to carry tubs of silage and tip it into the clean troughs ready for the cows when they came in for the afternoon milking, as we were given a tub we were told the name of the cow it was for, as the amount of silage varied as to how the cow was milking... During the afternoon milking I had a try, perched on a little stool with a bucket between my ankles, I tried a few tentative squirts, as I had been shown. The patient cow looked round at me, munched her silage and gave a long sigh, as if to resign herself to yet another learner... We spent our evenings reading, writing letters, washing, ironing or sitting round the fire talking about our homes, our families, our boyfriends and singing. So ended my first day in the Land Army. I rolled into bed in my underwear and took a leaf out of Sylvia's book. I dread to think what my mam would have thought of me!

To be able to milk a cow on a cold winter's morning is a nice warm experience. I used to lean my head against her flank, the milk would start to flow and I got a steady rhythm going. The milk makes a different sound when it first hits the bottom of the bucket—by the time you have a gallon or more it becomes a rich whooshing sound. If you have milked well there is a good froth on top of the warm milk. As I got more experienced I got a bit mischievous—the farm cats would sit on the other side of the gutter across from the cows. With a well aimed backward squirt of the cow's teat you could reach the cats. Some were good at catching the milk in their mouths, some even stood up on their back legs, open mouthed, to get the milk. If they missed, well they sat there washing their bibs till next time.'

Joan Law went to an agricultural college at Penkridge, near Wolverhampton:

'I remember it was a feeling of excitement and fear when I alighted from the train, a van was waiting to transport us to this beautiful mansion in lovely grounds. I remember thinking as we entered the hall and I saw the magnificent wide polished oak staircase, it was more fitted for debutantes to walk down in white dresses and satin slippers, than the heavy shoes we were issued with.

Then came our first night out in our uniform. We were being given a lift into Wolverhampton, in a lorry. My breeches were so tight around my knees I managed to get my foot on the wheel hub then they had to haul me in by the seat of my pants and ended up in a heap—most undignified. At the end of the month we were allowed home for the weekend. I was going to arrive home like a war hero, instead I looked a sorry sight carrying my kit bag, limping so badly I ended up carrying my shoes. My feet were so swollen. My mother spent the weekend trying to soften the leather shoes we had been issued with, never had my feet been so harshly treated.'

Joan's training for general farming started thus:

'We rose at 5.30 a.m., drank tea with no milk or sugar, but who cared at that time in the morning? Then off we went to our allotted tasks. My first encounter with a cow was off-putting to say the least. We had to wash their udders. My cow was a right comic, first she tried to squash me against the bars, and then I tried to milk her and both me and the stool landed in the slurry pit, smelling less than a rose. I never did get the hang of milking by hand. I was so glad my next week was in the fields, pulling beet, thought it would be a doddle, started off fine. By the time I got to the end of the row the beet was stronger than I. My head spun and I thought I would never straighten my back again. By the time we knocked off that night my hands were so sore and swollen I couldn't hold anything, let alone a pen to write home with. I just fell into bed and howled and wondered what on earth I had let myself in for.'

Doreen Leibrandt began her training by being sent to Usk Agriciltural College:

'...where I learned a lot about tractors. My first action on leaving home and moving in with eleven other girls in the dormitory was to get rid of my vests and buy myself some bras! I also stopped wearing my spectacles as being long-sighted I found they were not needed "en voyage".

The first and most important lesson of my Land Army career was learnt here, when mucking out cows, never stand behind one with a cough!

It was here that the reality of the country life was to come home to me, being sent out to gas foxes. I came upon a vixen and her three cubs playing in the early morning sunshine. The colours of the fur has always stayed with me as have the feelings of guilt at what we did to them.'

Olive Pettitt was sent to Suffolk, arriving on a lovely April day.

I was a real townie and had no idea what I was in for, just imagined a few peaceful cows in a meadow. The reality was a real shock when we found there were 87 cows of all breeds and we were expected to milk them, also clean out the cowsheds, not forgetting carting the milk to the dairy and all the washing of the utensils. Anyway, after a month's training, during which I was being sick every day for a week owing to smells of the cow muck and the milk, also chapped hands as we had to scrub the cowshed walls and I didn't ever dry them properly. We eventually got hardened to it all and began to enjoy it all a bit.'

Brenda Golden, too, learnt things she never needed:

'I can't say the month's training taught me a great deal although it was great fun and I kept in touch with a fellow trainee until a few years ago... I learned to horse plough which I never needed again and also sat on a sheep's head during a difficult lambing. During the ploughing the carter noticed the sheep in trouble, sent me to find the shepherd who was away somewhere and so the carter did what was necessary and we left the sheep and lamb quite happy with the rest of the flock.'

Doris Hall was being trained for horticulture.

'The head gardener showed me a small paddock, with the words, "I want this dug," and showed me how by turning over two spadefuls. I was then on my own. It took a week and I felt I was fully trained in digging! ... After the first week he proceeded to "train" me by helping him to fell the Colonel's Scots pines. The gardener himself was about 80.'

Enid Roffey comments on a period of training at the Plumpton School of Agriculture in East Sussex:

'Four weeks to learn the whole of the farming industry!'

Betty Jackson also trained at Plumpton:

'We worked from five in the morning until 5.30 p.m. for dairy and milking, seven in the morning until five in the evening when doing general farming. A canvas bag on a stand full of water with rubber teats was how I first learned to milk. My first encounter with a milking cow was at five o'clock in the morning in a dimly lit cowshed, to say I was scared is putting it mildly! My general farming included putting a barbed wire fence around Plumpton race course to keep the cows in while grazing.'

Audrey Wiitta and her friend Peggy were sent to a farm in Norfolk, the driver of the train had to be asked before leaving London to stop at this particular halt and when it did so, apparently miles from anywhere, the girls had to be lowered to the ground by other passengers as the drop was too great to negotiate without help. (Harrods Needlework department must have seemed a long way away.) Once on the farm "training" commenced and Audrey has vivid memories of the pair of them being sent to clean out pig styes hitherto untouched by hand. Since the smell was apalling they decided that gas masks were a good idea; unforunately Peggy had forgotten to rub soap on the mica and her mask was soon steamed up and because she couldn't see forked the muck in the general direction of Audrey, who was then to fork it outside. With Peggy's poor vision Audrey was soon plastered with muck and even after bathing and hair washing the smell lingered, not even overcome by copious applications of Californian Poppy (remember that?).

Barbara Youngman joined with a friend and they were sent to an agricultural college in Sussex for six weeks:

'What a shock—up at 5 a.m. every morning, 4 a.m. if it was your turn to "do horses". Never having been near a Shire, let alone groom it, I couldn't get over the size of their feet, let alone their bodies but oh, those lovely big brown eyes!'

Gladys Sirs' initial posting for training was to Leaden Roding, a tiny village deep in mid-Essex, for initiation to dairy farming:

'How well I remember the journey down to my new employers! It was a glorious day, I was feeling anything but glorious, travelling to Chelmsford the county town with both parents, having lunch at an hotel which featured boiled beef on the menu (made even more salty by the tears which dropped on to the plate), before setting out on the last stage of the journey. What a royal welcome awaited us on arrival at the farm—this was country hospitality at its very best, and we were all quickly made to feel like one of the family. Indeed, such was the good farmer's concern for the "new girl" from London that my parents were invited to visit the following weekend to see me and have a report on my progress caring for a mixed herd of Friesians and Dairy Shorthorns.'

Elizabeth Hanmer was called up and asked to attend Craibstone College of Agriculture north of Aberdeen for four weeks training:

'By the second week I found myself in charge of 400 pigs. The noise at feeding times must have exceeded the decibel tolerance of the present day! It made one hurry simply to shut them up.'

Helen Sheppard was sent for training to a farm in Smardon, Kent, with three other girls:

'The accommodation and food were dreadful. It was my first introduction to a pub—we were so hungry we bought crisps!'

Betty Venn who reported to the Agricultural College at Cannington where she learned to milk, found some memorable moments:

'We had to be at the farm at 5.30 a.m. after a big mug of hot milk. The walk was beautiful, thick frost on everything, the moon was full, we were wide awake by the time we reached the farm.'

Margaret Bodman, too, had a mile and a half to walk to work at 4 a.m.:

'Cold February morning... snow on the ground, moonlight helped us see our way across the fields. We found our alarm clock unreliable, so generally had to set it for 3 a.m. so we were not late. Walked home to breakfast, often fell asleep over the meal (potato cakes burnt outside and raw inside, as landlady did not know the time of our coming home), back to work, home for dinner, back in afternoon—nine miles a day. Felt bulky in new uniform—shown what to wear by experienced land girl. No coat issued at first, so had to borrow a friend's. Training lasted four weeks, divided between dairy work, general, calves and milking. Filled milk bottles, slow and very nearly let the milk run over till fellow land girl turned off a tap and saved the day. Milked first cow right out, a Jersey who kept shifting about as there was a cat in the walkway. Had to feed the bulls, one day I accidentally threw the bucket and all into the pen, so decided I had better climb the rails and retrieve it—bull was OK... Shared with Dorothy who is still my friend. We bought broken biscuits from the village shop, and kept them in a drawer. Did washing under cold tap in yard.'

Vera Campbell trained at an agricultural college which, she says:

'...did help in breaking us in but was very little use when we were posted, e.g. we were trained to machine milk and tractor maintenance etc. then landed in farms where no electricity, no tractors, just Clydesdales.'

Joyce Sansom was sent to the Chadacre Agricultural College in Suffolk for training:

'The first job was to groom the cart horses, not tail end we were told, go to the head and start there and never turn your back on a horse. I enjoyed it and learnt a lot, unfortunately I was then sent to a market gardener and had to hand pull nettles, not knowing they stung!'

Joyce Whiteley, who had asked for the Timber Corps, also received a month of training, and was sent to Culford Suffolk to join an intake of 100 London girls.

'We were in an army type camp... for a delicately nurtured, naive maiden like me, this was in itself a very exciting adventure, not to say an eye-opener in more ways than one. During the first week we were sent to try out a different branch of forestry every day. I went first to the sawmill. Using circular saws, from enormous ones which sliced into huge trunks, to tiny ones making half-inch batten, we learnt what to do and particularly how to finish the day with the right number of fingers on each hand!

The next day we learnt the work of a measurer. This was a responsible job as a good measurer made sure that a felled tree was put to the best possible use, with the least amount of wood wasted. She it was who decided which trunks were to go to the sawmill, and which were suitable to be made into pit-props for use in the coal mines, marking the latter to show where cuts had to be made. To be of any use, a pit-prop had to be the same width at the top and bottom to support its length. To aspire to be "passed out" at the end of the month as a measurer one had to be 19 years old at least—I was too young, much to my disappointment!

The following day we learnt how to saw the felled timber into the pit-props, cutting where the measurer had made her mark. We used "bushman" saws, two of us at a time, finding out very quickly how to place the trunks so that the cuts did not close up on the blade all the time. We found the sawing to be a very painful business as our muscles were so soft. We had to keep stopping all the time, and were glad to do some stacking to relieve our arms and backs. We felt that we had really contributed our share of "blood and sweat" to the war effort that day!

The day we were issued with axes and went felling was the most exciting day of all. I think mine weighed 4 lb and we learned how to sharpen them in the time-honoured way with a hand-held file and spit, and also on a foot-operated grindstone. As we hacked away at the poor trunks, trying not to cut off legs or toes (ours or anyone else's), we aimed at making nice open "mouths". When this had been achieved two of us knelt down, one each side of the tree, and with a huge cross-cut saw we sawed from the back towards the "mouth". In due course the tree fell but not necessarily quite where we expected. The shout of "timber" which went up was more a yell of trimphant relief than a warning to others, although this was also required. Those trees were no mere saplings and were quite some job to fell.

Then there was general forestry work. This was quite varied and did not require much brainpower. However, there was one vital skill involved, that of lighting a fire in a dripping wet wood! In the months to come when this was necessary, I was often called upon to blow life into a few glowing, but damp twigs. Having learnt deep breathing at singing lessons I was rather good at this—they called me "Bellows" on those occasions.

We used bill hooks to make the huge leafy branches into convenient sizes for the fire. The resultant conflagrations were enormous and many a baked potato charred and burst alongside the old black kettle. After this first week we were allotted to one type of work and I went to the sawmill for the next three weeks. At the end of the course our diplomas took the form of brass crossed-axes which were highly prized and quickly sewn on the sleeves of our overcoats. Then it was a case of "to the woods".

One thing I expect M. Smith had in common with Joyce in spite of training at Cannington Agricultural College:

'It was there that we ached from head to toe, all you could smell in our rooms was wintergreen and liniment.'

By contrast, Elizabeth Venner's experience at the School of Agriculture at Moulton seems almost idyllic:

'It was June, so the haymaking was in full swing. I had the job of driving a horse and hay rake across the field. Supposed to rake the hay into rows, but am afraid they were not very straight. We had three days on each section, pigs, learning to milk by hand, dairy work, picking blackcurrants, harvesting flax, so the month soon passed.'

Peggie George trained at Shipton Court, Shipton-under-Wychwood, as a market gardener:

'It was an amusing but happy month and we all slept in one big dormitory, just like school again! Some girls were doing farm training and only two of us gardening. We had to get up about 6.30 a.m. so took a glass of creamy Jersey milk to bed with us for the morning as no breakfast until 9 a.m. It was good training as the garden was superbly run. I still win prizes for my vegetables at our local village show. I never forget the first day I denuded the tomatoes of their leaves, as I had been asked to take the shoots out, and had never seen tomatoes actually growing before. The Head Gardener's face was a study, but he was very patient.'

Barbara Fowler was sent to Canfields Farm, Rudgwick for training, along with several other girls:

'There I was taught the art of hand milking the cows. I soon learned to dodge the restless legs that were bent on kicking me off my stool during my first fumbling attempts at relieving them of their milk. Meal times at first were quite an ordeal as being a nicely brought up suburban girl I was not used to the swarm of flies that continuously circled the table and quite often landed on the food. However, fresh air, hard work and long hours overcame my scruples and I was soon eating heartily with the rest.'

I. Jeffery went on a month's training course near Bridport in Dorset to learn to milk cows:

'I must say I did wonder why I had joined, as at 5.30 a.m. and pulling the cows' udders to try and get the milk out was a bit shattering. My hands ached for a week.'

The cows on which we learnt must have been a special breed! Just imagine getting used to one inexpert pair of cold hands when we started all over again with a fresh intake.

Marion Hinkley went for a month's training in the Weald learning to milk, strain, cool and bottle the milk:

'We had to get up at 4 a.m. to walk to work on time. Naturally there was no social life as we went to bed soon after our evening meal at 6 p.m.'

Joan Clifford was sent to Sparsholt Training Farm near Winchester for four weeks and received a travel warrant and a notice stating that during training, board and lodgings would be provided free and in addition there would be a personal allowance of 10/- (50p) a week, less National Health and Unemployment Insurance contributions:

'We were met at Winchester Station by an open lorry, there were six of us from London, and the rest from other parts of the country. We were put into a dormitory with, I think, six in each room. At Sparsholt we were up at 5 a.m. and allowed a cup of cold milk before milking. Then taught how to machine and hand milk... We had to clean the cowshed out with some of the largest and heaviest buckets and brooms I have ever used. It was my turn to fetch the cows down from the field, and in the dark early one morning I could just see one which would not come to my call at the top of the hill, so I went up to find out what was wrong. I felt so stupid—I had been calling a bush!

Our food rations were a pot of jam to last the month, a small bowl of sugar and a dish with our ration of butter and margarine to last the week (it never did!). All had labels with our names. One week our butter was rank and smelt awful—I was the first to go and complain and was given margarine in its place, then the rest of the girls went and had theirs changed too. We used to go into Winchester on our one half day and buy Marmite (which was not on points or rationed) and anything else we could "persuade" sympathetic shopkeepers to part with. Our parents sent cakes which we shared amongst our domitory. We always seemed to be so hungry!'

Neither Mary Vickery or her friend had had any experience of the land before and were complete 'greenhorns':

'We were sent to a farm to train with four other girls, this was quite an experience. The farmhouse was large and was run as a hostel (the manager and his wife were running it for the War Agricultural Committee) in that we had no curtains at the windows. Plenty of food which was very good. The first morning we went into the cowshed to try our hands at milking, not really knowing one end of the cow from the other. However, we both eventually managed to conquer the milking.'

Myra Hobden was sent to Sevenoaks, The Weald, to a hostel which housed about ten girls who came from around London and from all walks of life:

'the first morning we were called at 4.30 a.m. to start work at 5 a.m., no lateness was tolerated. It was quite dark at this time of the morning and we had a 15 minute walk. Just imagine walking into a shed of about 50 cows. I was terrified, but soon got to work with wheelbarrow, shovel and broom to "muck out".'

But Esme Hotchkiss's experience was probably unique:

'My first job was being tormented by a woman spiritualist who was supposed to train me to milk cows. I never want to meet another one!'

This page: 1, 2, 3 & 4. Harvest time. Joan Mant: 'The hardest, dirtiest job you can imagine, but lovely to see the results of so much hard work! And how did so much chaff work its way under one's clothes?'

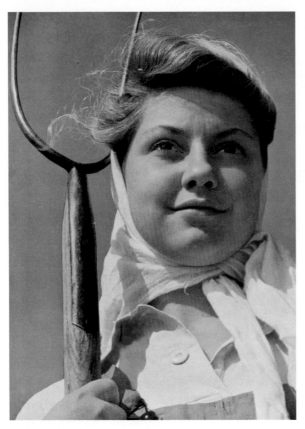

This page: 5, 6, 7 & 8. Harvest time.

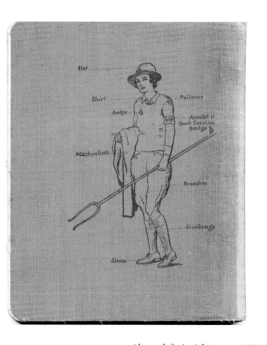

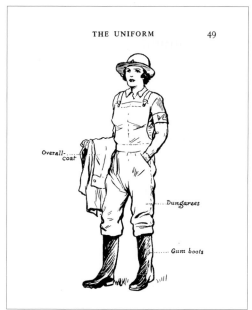

Above, left & right: 9 & 10. Land Girl uniforms. From a wartime Land Girl instruction manual.
Opposite page, right centre: 11. Part of the application form for joining the Women's Land Army.
Right: 12. Joan Mant in her Land Girl uniform.

This page: 13, 14, 15 & 16. The Land Army Timber Corps at work. Joan: 'I was not in the Timber Corps but Nelly and I were told to "go and cut up that wood"! You know the secret? You don't both push at the same time!'

No. 3

*

RELATIVE WORK-OUTPUTS OF WOMEN

according to the report prepared by J. H. Smith, M.Sc., Dept. of Agricultural Economics, University College of Wales, Aberystwyth

(*Output of adult male = 100*)

	Relative work output		Relative work output
TENDING LIVESTOCK:		POTATO CROP:	
Poultry	101	Planting (setting)	95
Milking	91	Lifting (picking)	91
Cattle	72	Weeding	75
FIELD WORK WITH HORSES:		Riddling and sorting	85
Driving hay mower	80	Sacking	61
Horse raking	71	Loading	44
Rolling	71		
Carting	69	OTHER ROOT CROPS:	
Harrowing	68	Hoeing beet and turnips	77
Ploughing	65	Lifting swedes and turnips	70
Odd jobs	62	Lifting mangolds	68
TRACTOR WORK:			
Driving, excluding repairs	73	MARKET GARDENING:	
Driving and repairs	49	Planting brassicas	90
LOADING AND SPREADING DUNG:		Cutting cabbage	83
		Bagging and netting cabbage	81
Loading	46	Pulling peas	103
Spreading	58	,, broad beans	96
HOEING AND WEEDING:		,, runner beans	101
Hoeing: general	75		
Weeding: general	88	COMMERCIAL HORTICULTURE:	
corn (miscell.)	79		
wheat	84	Cutting flowers	106
barley	84	Bunching ,,	106
HARVEST OPERATIONS:		Packing ,,	101
Turning hay	92		
Self-binding	51	FRUIT PICKING:	
Stooking	63	Plums	99
Loading sheaves	61	Apples	95
Rick work: hay	67	Cherries	95
corn	64	Small fruit	100
Threshing: general	70		
cutting bands	91		

NOTE.—It should be understood that these percentages apply to the typical women in agriculture and not only to members of the W.L.A.

G

Right: 17. Relative work outputs of women in comparison to men, report prepared *c.* 1944.
Below: 18. Farmer's report form. Assessment of a Land Girl's performance was quite bureaucratic.

FARMER'S REPORT

W.L.A. No. .... Name ....

1. Date on which training started ....

2. Did you find this volunteer
   (1) Strong enough for farm work ....
   (2) Handy ....
   (3) Willing and anxious to learn ....

3. While on your farm has she received instruction in :—

   Dairy work .... No. of Cows trainee can milk ....
   Poultry ....
   Care of Livestock ....
   Field Work ....
   Market Gardening ....

4. Please add any further remarks about the volunteer.

Signature of Farmer ....

37

LAND GIRL

A MANUAL FOR VOLUNTEERS
IN THE WOMEN'S LAND ARMY

W.E. SHEWELL-COOPER

ENGLISH UNIVERSITIES PRESS 1/-net

Left: 19. Front cover of commercially produced manual for Land Girls first published in 1941. It was intended to be a practical guide for the city slickers who were recruited into the Women's Land Army.
Below, left and right: 20. & 21. Land Girls were expected to operate heavy machinery as well as standard farm tractors. Joan: 'Machinery was unbelievably heavy to handle and sometimes a cause of accidents.'

This page: 22, 23, 24, 25 & 26. Land Girls cared for all manner of livestock including sheep. Joan: 'The girls were particularly good with livestock – except when it was time to send the calves to market.'

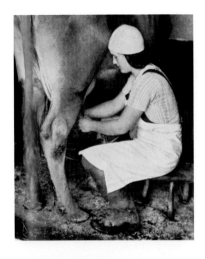

Left & Above: 27 & 28. Land Girls milking. Joan: 'Hand-milking of course but a lovely job and the cows never complained about the cold hands in winter time!'

Left & Above: 29 & 30. Tending calves and horses.

Left & Above: 31 & 32. Hens and swine!

Above left & right: 33 & 34. Work in the Land Army was hard. Digging ditches.

Above left & right: 35 & 36. Muck spreading. Joan: 'A little muck seemed to go such a long way.'

37. Carting sacks of potatoes. Joan: 'Sacking and carting potatoes – a really very heavy job and no-one taught us how to do it properly.'

Left: 38. Ploughing with horses.
Below & Bottom of page: 39 & 40. Treading the silo. One stage in the making of ensilage, a method of preserving green fodder. Joan: 'Treading the silo was not a bad thing at all – except for climbing in and out.'

Above & right: 41 & 42.
Land Girls laying hedges.
Joan: 'A well-laid hedge
was a lovely sight, really
something to show for all
the hard work.'

Top left: 43. In a west country orchard Land Girls gather plums, while rows of intercropped potatoes grow beneath the fruit trees.

Top right: 44. Land Girls tending salad crops in a market garden glass house.

Left: 45. Preparing ground for tomatoes in a greenhouse in the market-gardening country near Evesham.

The Land Army Song.   *Words and music both by Land-girls*

BACK TO THE LAND

Words by
P. ADKINS, W.L.A. 28299 & J. MONCRIEFF

Music by
E. K. LORING, W.L.A. 2053

1

Back to the Land, we must all lend a hand,
To the farms and the fields we must go.
There's a job to be done,
Though we can't fire a gun
We can still do our bit with the hoe.
When your muscles are strong
You will soon get along,
And you'll think that a country life's grand.
We're all needed now,
We must all speed the plough,
So come with us—Back to the Land.

2

Back to the Land, with its clay and its sand,
Its granite and gravel and grit,
You grow barley and wheat
And potatoes to eat
To make sure that the nation keeps fit.
Remember the rest
Are all doing their best,
To achieve the results they have planned
We will tell you once more
You can help win the war
If you come with us—Back to the Land.

Single copies 1d. each, 2d. post free, or 12 for 1s., post free, can be obtained from the Editor, "The Land Girl," Balcombe Place, Balcombe, Hayward's Heath, Sussex

46. Music and lyrics to *Back to the Land*, the Land Army song.

47. Delivering milk. Joan:'We were always welcome when delivering the milk, but the cry was always, "Is that all?"' Milk was rationed.

48. Putting down poison.

49. Ploughing a straight furrow.

W. L. A.
1939-50

THIS PLAQUE RECORDS THE
FARMERS' APPRECIATION
OF THE WORK
OF THE LAND GIRLS
IN WILTSHIRE
DURING WAR AND
PEACE

This page: 50, 51 & 52. Commemoration. Joan: 'The top illustration seems to say it all; the countryside, loneliness and "doing a man's job". The surviving women of the Land Army were finally officially recognised for their contribution to the war effort with a medallion issued in 2008. Hilda Gibson, 83, spent two years in the WLA killing rats in Lincolnshire before transferring to Norfolk to muck out and feed poultry. She said the badge was a "powerful and touching gesture to thank us for what we did". This is the authors.

7

ALL HANDS...

At the times when work on the land became even more labour intensive we were joined by local women, soldiers, prisoners of war, conscientious objectors and schoolboys. The schools had a week's holiday at the end of October known as the potato picking holiday. It is now more famously known as half term. The local women were used to the work and whilst we were still regarded with some suspicion eventually we all managed to work peaceably together.

It was, however, the differences in treatment between us and prisoners of war (POWs) and conscientious objectors (CO) that made us hopping mad and which we still remember. I recall working in the rain, quietly drowning, whilst COs took shelter. Some too were choosy about what they did whilst we had no choice, and Joyce Sansom:

'...dug ditches when the POWs refused to do it as did some COs.'

Dorothy Fox remembers taking strike action:

'We actually went on strike in October because we were being transported to work in open lorries, whilst Italian and German POWs were taken to work in covered ones, so we stayed away from work one Saturday morning and had 5/- docked from our pay, but we had covered lorries on the Monday morning! We worked with both German and Italian prisoners and some of the Italians had been in the war in Ethiopia in 1936 and had then been drafted to fight in North Africa, where they had been taken prisoners, so they hadn't been back to their homes for almost ten years. One of them came from Sicily and promised to send me perfume and oranges when he got back—needless to say, I'm still waiting! Also working on the land were Irishmen who had come over here to work and then went home for six months to avoid paying tax.'

I. G. Thompson, too, recalls the peculiarly insensitive treatment:

'One day we went—by lorry—to Slimbridge—raining hard—and we sloshed around picking the potatoes up and throwing them into the lorry—*our* lorry—while some Italian POWs who were supposed to be doing the same said it was too wet and were driven back to their camp *in a coach*, while we returned later to the hostel, in the same muddy lorry we'd used to collect the potatoes. A few blue words that night.'

In spite of these incidents, days spent in the open air working alongside each other brought amicable relationships and, as Gladys Levingbird says, we were a fine mixed bag:

'I had to pick up, and work with many different groups—"farming campers" mostly from London who worked on the farm for their holidays, Welsh miners who had a recuperating period of a few months to get the fresh air, civilian prisoners from Bedford jail—each lorry had a prison officer to guard them, and also RAF new recruits from Cardington Camp.'

Olive Black, working from a hostel, was among those picked up and taken to their destinations by girl lorry drivers:

'...where we sometimes worked alongside other quite interesting gangs comprising COs, German and Italian POWs and even prisoners from Holloway. Most interesting especially when they told us what they were "in for". They were much better off than us, they were able to stop at the slighest sign of rain, and always had portable loos.'

Time and again the girls comment on the differences between German and Italian POWs. Berta Gillatt worked with soldiers, timber fellers and POWs and says:

'Italian POWs made baskets and rings out of coins. Had some hair-raising situations with the Italian POWs—not so the German POWs, they kept their distance. Coming in contact the first time with a lorry full of Hitler's German Youth—how pitiful they looked. I thought is this really what the war has come to, children as POWs.'

Cynthia Banbury, too, noted the variations and couldn't help putting her spoke—or pitchfork—in:

'There were Germans at Morton and now Italians came each day by lorry. The Germans were much better workers, we thought, more skilful. We usually caught the Italians under the hedges in the fields when harvesting and gave them a little prick with a pitchfork... One German used to bring me his soap ration, Knight's Castile, because he saw me washing my hands with carbolic soap in the dairy.'

Vera Wakeling worked with both German and Italian POWs:

'It was interesting to see the difference in the way the nationalities reacted to their circumstances. The Germans were very resourceful and inventive, and one chap devised a way of making sandals from old tyres and discarded binder twine. He made me a handsome pair, the twine being dyed with beetroot juice.'

Sheila Gordon-Rae too noted the differences:

'Another picture that comes to mind is the Italian POWs singing at their work and always one of them cooking their pasta on a camp fire. The Germans were a different matter—no smiles from them! Unlike the Italians they were not glad to be out of the war.'

Joan Welbourn worked with German POWs:

'Once a week the WLA were invited to the camp to listen to concerts, the men were very talented. We were not allowed to fraternize with them, that was the rule, sometimes rules were broken, a packet of cigarettes would be passed over when you were bagging cabbages together.'

Margaret Hall, too, has pleasanter memories of German POWs:

'Apart from one or two who had been in the Gestapo, the boys were very friendly and we got on well. In fact, two of them returned after the war and married local girls.'

Joyce Murphy says how well the girls were treated by the German POWs as they worked together:

'...if it was our birthday they would make us a cake and carve something out of wood for us.'

Enid Ballard members kindness and cheerfulness from Italian POWS:

'...they sang a lot, gathered mushrooms and chestnuts and cooked them for us...'

Both Audrey Sykes and Doreen Leibrandt noted the lack of desire to escape by the POWs:

'Some of them were incredibly young, only sixteen years old, and glad to be out of the fighting. The Germans were good workers and were kept in order by Albert, their head man. Originally they had an armed guard with them but it was obvious none of them wanted to escape and return to the battle front, so later on they were dumped from a truck and collected at the end of the day. Some were country folk themselves and for years I had a large willow basket made by one of them, price 20 cigarettes.'

And

'...I found them very polite and helpful. What was both amazing and amusing was that these "prisoners" would walk for miles to and from work without any supervision. I remember one very large camp at Billingshurst being run by only a handful of "Tommies" to keep order.'

8

BOMBING

It was a common misconception that once we joined the Land Army we were removed from the immediate effects of enemy action, that is if you didn't count rationing and the fact that we were away from home worrying about families left behind. Nancy Johnson puts it in a nutshell:

'Many people seemed to think that because we worked on the land we escaped the horrors of war, but in my case I was near the Thames Estuary and in line for the bombing of London. Many months were spent sleeping in an air-raid shelter and many times I crouched down by the tractor or stood under a tree thinking I might get some protection from the bombs.'

Of course it depended on where you were posted. Vera Redshaw was first sent to Rochford, near Southend:

'It was during a period when there were many tip-and-run air raids around the Thames Estuary and one day a group of us were hedging and ditching when we heard machine gun fire overhead—some of it apparently very close. Our foreman told us to run for cover and the nearest place was a derelict stone barn. Nearby there were some conscientious objectors working in the fields and they also came running. They were members of the Lord's Peculiar People, a sect quite numerous in the area and known locally as The Peculiars. They didn't join us but went behind the dividing stone wall and proceeded to sing hymns. We were singing as a mark of defiance to the Germans and to keep from feeling jittery, but our repertoire included such things as *In the Mood*. Actually I don't know how much protection the barn afforded as there was no roof on it...

While stationed in Rochford I went with two other girls who, like me, were in private billets, to the pictures in Southend. It was Saturday night and the buses ran a little later than usual. Towards the end of the film the purple siren went. We were anxious to know how the film ended so we hung hung on until the yellow warning, when we decided we ought to go. As we got to the bus stop the driver was calling "Come on, this'll be the last bus to Rochford." Sure enough, by the time we arrived there the AA guns were blasting away and shrapnel was dropping all round me. One of the three, Evelyn, was from a little village in the West Riding where they hadn't even experienced the nightly gunfire which was had in Leeds, my home town, every night, and she was in quite a state. As we were running past a row of houses she said, "Quick, in here, I know these people." We knocked at the door and were duly let in. There were no lights on in the house as their blackout was faulty... the three of us sat on the settee in total darkness and made conversation. It suddenly struck me that if we saw these people again we wouldn't recognise them and here we were sitting demurely on their settee. I started to giggle and the three of us shook silently stifling our mirth. When the All Clear went and we were let out of the house we said to Evelyn, "Well, at least you know who they were," to which she replied, "Don't know them from Adam—just panicked and made up the story about my landlady knowing them."

We were surrounded by bomber crews from all over the Commonwealth. Three crews in particular used to regard the hostel as a second home and would come and sit round the slow combustion stoves laughing and talking during the evening, but none of these crews survived and many days were spent in tears as well as laughter, and some days were very difficult to get through when the sun was shining brightly but the days seemed dark.'

Audrey Wiitta told me with still a trace of bitterness:

'We spent all day getting the harvest in, the German Air Force spent all night trying to set it alight. Each morning we went out to spot the incendiaries for local soldiers to come and remove.'

Audrey travelled to the market garden where she worked by workmen's train and one early morning with the bombers overhead the train drew to a stop, close behind another. A fellow passenger pushed her to the floor, under the seat, and the other train was bombed. She arrived at work two hours late, black from head to foot, to find her fellow land girls in tears as they had heard about the raid on the train and presumed she was a casualty. She still lost two hours' pay for late arrival!

Daphne Stone too, was in the South East:

'Whilst at the farm we had our first taste of aerial attack from "sneak" raiders which flew across the Channel under the cover of cloud and dived low, peppering the village with bullets; or sometimes a squadron of enemy bombers, limping home, would jettison a few remaining bombs at random. On one occasion Peggy and I were clearing the remains of the harvest in the field alongside the race-course, when a plane zoomed out of the clouds and seemed intent upon attacking us. To get to the safety of the farmhouse we had to hoist ourselves over the fences on either side of the course, and in our panic, found ourselves hooked on to the fences by our dungarees!

But the most exciting, though moving, event was the epic Dunkirk Rescue. That beautiful day—calm with a cool mist—we were working once more in the field by the railway line at Westernhanger. It was usual for troop trains to pass through from Folkestone to London with passengers (mostly army personnel) leaning out of the windows with cries of "Hi, blondie!" wolf whistles and the like. But that day, several trains passed through in absolute silence and Peggy and couldn't think why, until we noticed that they were full of khaki-clad figures with bandaged heads and limbs, accompanied by Red Cross personnel, and later we learned that they were the survivors picked up by the "little ships" that had gone out from Folkestone and Hythe to assist the evacuation of Dunkirk.'

Marguerite Woodcraft lived at home and worked in greenhouses near Chingford:

The bus journey used to be quite hectic at times with doodlebugs around, and many a time the conductor of the bus shouted out to us to sit on the floor when he thought danger was imminent. This reminds me of the time in the greenhouses when a doodlebug cut out, giving us time to jump into the ditches. Most of the glass in the greenhouses was shattered when the explosion occurred—one of the workers, a man in his late fifties, was deaf and he didn't hear the doodlebug. He was shocked when glass fell all round him but luckily didn't get cut.'

Mary Becraft, too, was working in greenhouses growing tomatoes:

'While a raid was on we used to carry on working as a lookout was on duty. My last memory of that place was a shout from the lookout, dashing out of the glass house and seeing this huge black doodlebug hovering towards us. Mrs Rumsey showed us into the shelter and to this day I can still hear the sound of crashing glass.'

Yvonne Timbs was in Kent when the doodlebugs started to arrive:

'I recall one of my friends said when she heard them coming, "They sound like a motor bike," and when the engine stopped we knew it was coming down. Kathy used to put her head in the haystack, with the rest of her sticking out, we often put her tin hat on her bottom. One of the girls got some shrapnel in her arm, not too serious. We used to watch our boys intercepting the doodlebugs, very spectacular... no matter where we were we just dropped to the ground and put our tin hats on and hoped for the best.'

The doodlebugs made us all twitchy and we all remember the eerie silence when the engine cut out. Margot Bettles was in East Sussex with a large gang doing field work:

'We were machine gunned by a German plane after it had dropped bombs on Eastbourne, and those awful doodlebugs coming down in the very field we were working in.'

Olga Tremayne, whilst in training at Limpsfield Lodge saw the first doodlebug that came over Britain:

'It landed in Croydon at 7 a.m. We were milking then of course and we wondered what this curious thing was... We soon found out and the area was filled with balloons, one being in our adjoining field. It was a strange feeling on the first night to go out in our tin hats to the ditch when the first warning came... the balloons were trying to bring the doodlebugs down before they reached Croydon and London and we thought for sure we would be killed that night. We were amazed when the first doodlebug escaped the balloons' wires and we were in and out all night with "Warnings" and "All Clears"! We didn't bother after that but ack-ack was pretty lively and poor old Oxted soon didn't have many windows left... We would watch the fighter planes with mixed feelings chasing the doodlebugs, as they would be in danger of being blown up themselves.'

Joan Baker, working near the Woolwich Arsenal and the docks experienced her fair (or unfair?) share of air raids:

'We had air-raids and the flying bombs were in full force and we were in the corridor from the launching sites across Kent into London. Our nearest escape was when working outside and a flying bomb seemed to cut out right above us. It exploded about a quarter of a mile away and the blast would have knocked us flat except that we were already flat on the ground. It landed on a housing estate made up of wooden temporary pre-fab huts built in the First World War. We also attracted the attentions of a simple minded flasher who became such a regular feature that the Head Gardener had to call in the police who warned him off.'

Margaret Bodman, too, mentioned that silence when the engine cut out:

'Doodlebug alley, RAF balloons brought down 25 flying bombs within a two mile radius, seven of which landed on the farm. Jumped into ditch when we heard them. Allowed to join the family in their indoor Morrison shelter. On hearing a V1 we counted up to seven, then the bang—we're safe.'

That count of seven must have seemed endless. Peggie George remembers the hazards of flattening oneself during a raid:

'The old gardener (Charley) and I got on famously together. We were working in the field one day when we heard a bomb. Charley shouted, "Lie down, mate," and we threw ourselves on the ground, right in a bed of what proved to be nettles!'

Dealing with the blackout on a farm was irritating and time consuming as Isabel Newnham found:

'...I helped with the cowsheds. Thick cardboard was slotted over the windows and the light bulbs were changed to blue ones. Double entrances were made so that we—and the cows—could go in and out without showing a light. Then the dozens of notch holes in the walls had to be plugged with straw and when we'd finished not a chink of light could be seen. Next, the dairy windows had blackouts and it took quite a while to fix them at dusk and take them down in the morning... One night about two o'clock the siren went and we heard planes overhead... We rushed downstairs and got under the table. Being a round table with a thick centre leg we couldn't get far under, just our heads and shoulders. Only three rumps sticking out and in my terror I could imagine where the shrapnel would strike first. It might even have brought a smile to Jerry's face had he seen us. After a few seconds we heard three sickening thuds as a stick of bombs fell. It happened that the three bombs had straddled the farm narrowly missing the main railway line that ran alongside and no doubt that was what was aimed at... As time went on the war situation worsened and air-raids became a nightly occurrence... We often heard the shrapnel fall on the tin roofs of the cowsheds.'

Gladys Foster writes calmly of her experiences but I don't suppose she felt as placid at the time:

'One night whilst an air-raid was in progress and we were sheltering in a barn (goodness knows why we had to go out there when there was a perfectly good Morrison shelter indoors) we saw a shadowy figure of a man in the orchard. The bailiff said, "Oh, that's only Mr C—one of the farm labourers," but it turned out to be a German airman who had baled out of his plane. Apparently he walked across the fields to the nearest village and was discovered sitting on the church wall. We also saw one of the first doodlebugs and thought it a peculiar looking thing with flames coming out of its tail, it came down not far from Canterbury. The sight I shall never forget was the convergence of Allied planes going over to liberate Europe, the sky was absolutely full of them as far as the eye could see and it lasted for ages. We were told that the cauliflowers we were cutting and bagging were for airlifting to Holland to relieve their food shortage.'

I remember being machine gunned by a 'stray'—it's an experience likely to stay in one's mind and leave one wondering at the turn of speed which could be produced to reach shelter. Christine Bailey had afternoon milking disrupted in this way:

'I was rounding up the cows one Sunday early afternoon ready for milking, and German fighter planes flew in low over the coast and started machine gunning everything in sight. I was lucky again not to be hit and no cows were hurt, but it was a nasty experience.'

Sylvia Dean Cawley, near Manston aerodrome, tells of a safe landing:

'Also once while at the top of a tree there was a flash of lightning, and a plane's engine overhead stopped and it seemed ages coming into sight. Fortunately the airman parachuted down and landed on the marshes, the plane crashing near him... We often witnessed injured planes coming back and landing badly, or as they said "on a wing and a prayer".'

Marion Hinkley mentions the dog fights taking place:

'There was quite a lot of action overhead with "dogfights" and later the first jet planes trying to shoot down the flying bombs before they reached London. Many times a beautiful formation of Flying Fortresses would pass over only to return later struggling with ominous gaps.'

Gwen Lawrence:

'My most vivid memory was seeing a German bomber trying to get home and, as it flew low over our farm, watching the bomb doors open and the bombs dropping down on Milford. I also remember the night an ammunition train was bombed at Tongham. The bombs went off for hours after.'

Evelyn Jenkin remembers those who did not return from ithe invasion:

'The whole of SE England had troops under canvas waiting for the Normandy invasion. Sadly many never returned. One night they all quietly disapeared and the country was quiet and lonely without them.'

Chris Breeze, too remembers the departure of troops:

'In the evenings we would go into the village and singsong around the piano with the Americans, then one night they were all gone and it happened to be D-Day so they must have been there. The boats all went from Poole Harbour that night, our farmer watched them from the hill top.'

Doreen Leibrandt gives a vivid picture of D-Day:

'One of the great delights was watching the Sunderland flying boats leaving and ponderously returning from patrol to their station at Nayland Dock. This reminds me of one of my lasting memories, early one beautiful morning watching wave upon wave of bombers with their fighter escorts leaving vapour trails across the summer sky. We were all curious and wondered why and where they were going only to find out on the next news broadcast that D-Day had begun. It was in Haverfordwest one morning on the way to work that we discovered one of the most horrific episodes of the war. We were wondering why, on coming over the bridge and up the hill to the paper shop, everyone was standing transfixed reading their newspapers. Once we had returned to the van and opened our papers we were also shocked at the discovery of the Belsen and Auschwitz concentration camps.'

Ailsa Tanner recalls how conditions changed dramatically near Loch Fyne:

'They were using a large sandy bay on Loch Fyne for manoeuvres, practising landings for D-Day in France, although we did not know that at the time. It was decided to move farms and all their stock further inland. To begin with Point was allowed to remain but received livestock from three small farms nearby... The army eventually took over the whole of Ardlamont and the dairy cows had to be taken inland near Kilfinan. That was when I had to leave...

It was a most beautiful night with a moon just one night over the quarter, a clear blue sky and stars. A barge started shooting while moving in towards Ostal Bay and the gun flashes were quite bright, then all the barges moved slowly into the bay itself and there were mysterious signals and flashing with searchlights.

The reason for the evacuation was that the army was using live ammunition, and though some young stock was left to graze, and did suffer some casualties, every other human and farm animal had to leave.

Shortly before this the other land girl, Ella, and I discovered two parachutes in the water near the shore and reported them to the Home Guard. This led to an entertaining display on a Sunday afternoon for the farm children, Peter and ourselves, and Donald the Post all perched on the rocks of Craigmore. Round the Point came a naval vessel, it did not come in too close as magnetic mines were suspected, but a small party came ashore in a wooden dinghy, with a young lieutenant in charge... to our amazement this youth took off his jacket, his waistcoat, his trousers, and so on till he was stark naked, and most courageously plunged into the far-from-warm sea. He dived into the waves to have a look under the water and his pink behind rose majestically into the air each time! Then he swam back and said it was too dark, he could see nothing. The poor lad was chittering with the cold wind. His colleague gave him his jersey to dry himself andf he had difficulty putting on his uniform as his skin was sticky.

Naturally we heard no more about this at the time, but many years later, coming back from Colonsay on the ferry, the purser happened to mention that his father had been skipper of the naval vessel, and the parachutes were attached to magnetic mines. He could not take my word that I had been there, and wanted to know my farmer's name as proof positive!'

Not all frights from the air came from enemy action as Julia Porteous recounts:

'I once got a terrible fright with a very low flying plane that came over the byre while we were milking. The machines were kicked off by the cows and they were all in a state of shock and the calves broke out and ran wildly up the field. It turned out to be an American pilot saluting his fiancée who was the schoolmaster's daughter. He did not think of the commotion and fright he gave everyone as we did not know if it was the Germans or not. There was an apology from him in the local paper the next week.'

On a lighter note, listen to Barbara Ould:

'Every time I watch *Dad's Army* I think of a man I worked with—Bill Smith. One Sunday morning I was cycling from my digs to early communion at the village church—reaching the bottom of the hill met Bill Smith in uniform standing guard—*bayonet fixed* telling me, "You can't go this way, land mines have dropped." When I asked to see them he pointed to five chalked rings in the road! He just wouldn't let me pass, so I had to cycle all the way up the hill, down the other side and I was late for church. *But* I gave him hell the next morning!'

There was, too, the threat of invasion and the September 1941 issue of *The Land Girl* gave instructions entitled 'In the Event of Invasion', telling farmers and farm workers it was their first duty to go on producing every ounce of food possible—'... ploughing, cultivating, sowing, milking, hoeing and harvesting, just as if no invasion were occurring... Tractors and motor vehicles will be needed to carry on the farm work but must be put out of action if they are in real danger of capture by the enemy. To do this, remove and hide well away the distributor head and leads and either empty the petrol tank or remove the carburettor—if a diesel engine remove the injection pump and connection... milk, perishable fruit and vegetables should be sold to those nearby and given away when necessary... Farm workers must be on duty on the farm all day and every day until the military or the police order otherwise.'

However, an end did come and here are two different reactions. First Dorothy Fox:

'We heard at the beginning of May that the war in Europe had ended, we were working on a farm near the River Usk, so we all downed tools and went for a swim in our undies! The foreman at the depot ticked us off but said he wished he'd been there!'

And Ann Bibbings:

'When all the harvest was carried one of the men would thatch the ricks with the help of one or two girls, whose job it was to draw the thatch in, in other words, straighten the straw. I was doing this job when the war ended and we plaited a V sign at the end of each rick.'

9

THESE YOU HAVE LOVED—OR NOT

We were young, away from home and into a new life. Those girls who worked with us, moaned with us, laughed and shared our confidences, will always be remembered, whether or not we are still in touch. I remember my workmates as still young—where are you now Mag, and what about Roma and Teddie, Landia the Valkyrie, and Nellie the nippie, and what was the name of the dark-haired brown-eyed robin of a girl at Limpsfield who said to me one evening, 'Coo, you ain't arf a bleedin' corfdrop'?

Our landladies, too, were memorable, most looked after us, laughed with us and listened tolerantly to our tales of woe. Others, of course, are remembered for different reasons!

We had not, however, anticipated the attitude of the men and women we worked with. Employing girls, town girls at that, was, I was told, 'going agin nature'. This was not entirely true since local girls and women had always been employed seasonally, but we were different. We wore a uniform for a start which set us a little apart, and we came mostly from towns and therefore we were 'fast'. When I protested at being called 'fast' I was told, 'Well, you comes from Lunnon, don't you?'—end of argument. There was also the way we did things; land girls working together laughed and sang, and the songs from those years bring memories crowding back. Play *You Are My Sunshine* to a gathering of ex-Land Army girls and we are away! It must, however, be said that by working hard at it we were usually accepted in the end. As Evelyn Waight remembers:

'The older men on the farm resented us very much and there were a few scenes and grafitti on carts etc. but eventually when the farm was sold these same men were in tears as we shook hands with them.'

Audrey Manning recalls:

'After four weeks' training I felt as if I had been working on a farm all my life and I was ready to tackle any job. Some of the old hands doubted whether we'd stick it. We'd hear such scathing comments as, "What have they sent *you* for?" or "This ain't no job for you young gals, you won't be able to 'ave no babies". We used to go to dances in Meopham Village Hall. There was an officious woman on the door who would not allow land girls in if they were wearing uniform.'

Then there was the local sport of taking the rise out of 'them gels'. Barbara Ould says:

'When I joined the WLA it was early summer so hay-making started soon after. In those days hay wasn't put into bales but hay ricks were made and hay taken up by elevator. We had some difficulty in shaping the top of the rick as the elevator was too short and it was suggested that two sky hooks would do to take up the rest of the hay. I was told to go and get them from the top of the field—I went! I never have lived it down to this day—sky hooks! But I resisted when told to go and get a pint of pigeon's milk and as for the scythe with the seat on it...!'

As Connie McNichol says, we were objects of great interest among other farm workers:

'... most of whom were firmly convinced that because we came from Glasgow, we all lived in the Gorbals and had been brought up on fish and chips and tea. We were supposed to take our own sandwiches for midday but often we were invited to join the family and were given soup and a share of whatever else was going. We received the greatest kindness at the poorer farms, up in the Galloway hills when working from the hostel at Ken Bridge, near Galloway, whereas when working in the garden of a large house on a wealthy estate where there were two live-in land girls, we were shown to the potting shed for our midday break.'

Olive Pettitt tells how prejudice was overcome:

'At first the two cowmen resented us for being just two "gals". Wouldn't help us lift heavy sacks of food for the cows, but we dragged the sacks and wouldn't ask for help. In the end we all became good friends.'

Diana Powell has memories that have lasted over the years:

'...in the cold, wet weather when the men were working inside the barns the girls would be out in the fields—much to the amusement of the men.'

Surely it wouldn't have been quite so bad or so memorable if the men hadn't thought it funny?

But out of the gloom comes Mary Phipps with her golden memory:

'I had the afternoon off when they found out it was my 21st birthday. As I was coming back from town I was sitting with the village teacher, she made me take a small sponge cake she had bought, said she was sorry it wasn't a proper birthday cake. Proper choked I felt!'

Joan Law, too, has tales of kindness after being treated with resentment by the farm hands:

'We were sent to a farm near West Bromwich. We had already come across what to us was unexpected, that was the old farm hands really hated us, made life hard in every way they could, had some notion we would take their sons' jobs while they were away... At the bottom of the farm drive there was a colliery and we had permission to use their canteen. These hard-working men were real gentlemen. They treated us like royalty, never before or since have I been treated so well. Remembering everything was rationed and in short supply, when we went in the man serving would say, "Oh girls, I have got a little something put by for you," and from under the counter would come a jam tart or some such treat. Our mugs of tea, you could stand the spoon up in the sugar he put in. We hadn't the heart to tell him we were slimming. One day we were tackling a man-sized meal, when Andy decided she wanted the salt. While getting it she slipped with her hob-nailed boots on the stone floor. It was so funny almost before she hit the ground there was a mass exodus from the tables all diving to pick Andy up. There was only Elsie and I eating unconcerned... Also up the lane was waste land where the army tested the tanks. One morning Andy was late and we were getting bothered about her when up rolled a tank. It stopped and out got three soldiers, all three bent down the turret and hauled something out. It was Andy. They had given her a lift to work. She was deaf for three days.'

Evelyn Jenkin found that farm labourers swore a lot but didn't have much to say:

'...they certainly left us to do the heavy work, and anything they knew they kept to themselves.'

Molly Campbell puts the other side of the story:

'Looking back, one realises how hard it must have been for farmers to cope with raw girls from town backgrounds.'

and then goes on:

'Now I live in the country and know how mechanised farms have become, I realise just how primitive conditions were during the war. The girls worked hard, and at times the work was very hard indeed. Some of the men resented the girls. At one market garden gipsies and COs were employed as well as land girls. The gipsies gave the rest of us a very hard time, lazing about while the girls did the heavy lifting. Yet it must have been very galling to see how the girls larked about and laughed and enjoyed themselves while the men had families to keep on very low wages. Their wives had to take in washing, do housework for the employers, be "respectful"— forelock touching was a fact.'

Sometimes we thought our employers lived in another world—they probably and quite rightly thought we did. Evelyn Waight remembers one such employer:

'The following year after we joined, my sister and I were loaned out to a titled lady who had a country mansion and kitchen garden about seven miles from Dovercourt. We had to cycle there and back every day. For three months we slogged around, looking after tomatoes, picking strawberries, currants (red, white and black), beans, spinach and making hay of the lawns. We were at her beck and call and received the occasional cup of cocoa, got bitten by her unruly dogs and when we left (at our own request) she was quite hurt but said that we did deserve some reward and gave us a jar of homemade raspberry jam!'

Gladys Sirs remembers a very kind employer though there was a fly in the ointment:

'My next posting was to another dairy farm about 10 miles distant featuring Red Polls, where once again I received the same kindness and consideration from my employer, a most charming Scottish lady. Regretfully, however, an unfortunate incident involving the farm foreman (an unpleasant type of person making very unwelcome advances) made my stay rather short. In fact about six weeks... I can still taste those delicious Scotch pancakes, but more importantly I remember her kindness in making certain that I would be placed in a suitable position before moving on.'

Joy Morgan shows clearly where her sympathies were:

'Farmers on the whole treated us like second class citizens and their wives were very jealous of us. A land girl had to have very broad shoulders and a terrific sense of humour. I remember one gentleman (tongue in cheek) farmer who lived in luxury but treated his staff like slaves. I lodged with his general labourer and family in his tied cottage. No electricity or proper sanitation. The children only had one pair of shoes for going to school so went barefoot the rest of the time. I gave up wearing my shoes around the place so as not to embarrass them... After I left I heard he sacked the labourer and threw the family out of the house. He deserved horse whipping. I nearly hit him with my hoe once when he was beating the young girl. I'm sure there were some nice farmers around and I was just unlucky... One lady in Marazion I was billeted with, looked like a witch and used to dabble with the spirits. She used to scare us nearly out of our wits but made up for this with the lovely Cornish pasties she would make. They were enormous.'

Elizabeth Hanmer's farm manager seems to have had a rare problem with his land girls:

'Naturally we were treated with great suspicion by many of the rather elderly farmworkers, however they were never unkind so far as I can remember. I do remember the farm manager we were working under. He was unbearably shy. He couldn't look us in the face at all, and our daily orders were given us in an almost inaudible mumble in broad Scots as he stared at his boots. After he had gone there was usually a discussion beginning with, "What did he say about...?" We were lucky if one of the men was with us to translate the mumblings of his boss.'

Elsie Druce remembers with affection the 'characters' she met on the farm:

'We had a variety of characters working for the squire, one of whom was Willie Foddler. He was about 60, lived with his tiny sister, two years younger and she also did all the jobs on the farm. But Willie especially was the horse man. He was in charge of two huge, perfectly matched black shires, Charlie and Chance. Even if the horses were just going out to cart muck, as long as they were going through the village the harness gleamed and their hooves were blackened and shining.

There were other horses and horse woman Aggie Hall worked these. I wrote to Aggie till she died in 1979, she shares the same churchyard as the famous Grace Darling. In my eyes Aggie was just as famous. Old Mr Dixon was 83 or thereabout, he owned his own small farm with his son. Mr Dixon rode an old bike everywhere. It had no brakes at all so there was no stopping the thing, he would yell for everyone to watch out, then he would run it on and up an incline and when it stopped he just fell off.'

Many of us who worked on dairy farms also undertook milk delivery, some by van, others on bikes—I walked, lugging a heavy can. I was met at the doors by someone tendering a jug and I would measure out the milk—I loved this part of the day and was usually made welcome. The best part would be the last stop of all, at the local bakery, the wonderful smell of fresh bread and George and Charlie covered in flour—wielding a large teapot. George would always ask, 'Long tea or short tea?' and I discovered that long tea meant holding the teapot about two feet above the cup and short tea meant holding it about six inches above. If it was a wretched morning I was sometimes sent outside to the bus stop to ask if any of the waiting passengers would like a cup, and it often developed into a sort of party.

Enid Dalloway too had a milk round:

'There were some funny moments. Like the mornings I used to collect the money from an elderly couple, brother and sister I believe they were, in East Street as the road used to be called, and always the money was put ready on the breakfast table along with the bread and marmalade only placed right beside a set of false teeth! It gave me the horrors, but I had to pick up the money, I don't know whether I expected the teeth to bite me or perhaps it was that I never could stand looking at false teeth like that, grinning at me.

Another customer from whom I had to go in and collect money was an elderly lady who was bedridden, now I didn't mind walking through the kitchen and into her bedroom but for the fact that she had an Aga cooker that seemed to belch forth the most ghastly coke fumes. It was terrible, really choking fumes they were. I used to take a deep breath as I reached the back door and rush in to pick up the money hoping that the lady might be asleep and I could make a quick retreat. Of course, nine times out of ten she was wide awake and ready for a little chat. I really don't know how she survived so long in that choking atmosphere, poor soul.

Several of my customers were kind enough to offer me cups of coffee or tea on my daily round which were mostly very welcome providing I didn't spend too long drinking them and making myself late getting back to the farm, and of course in cold weather too many drinks could become a problem when there was nowhere to spend a penny till I got back.

I met so many nice people amongst my customers. My favourite was Annie, and on my very first morning when I delivered her milk she was so friendly that I looked forward to seeing her each morning. At that time her youngest daughter had been evacuated and now Annie was expecting her home very shortly and she talked so much about her little Grace. Annie was the sort of person who made you feel so welcome to the village and I know it was because of people like her that I settled in so quickly and never felt like a "foreigner". There was Mrs Turner, she very often had a cup of coffee ready for me and on baking day would usually provide a bun or a sponge finger to eat with it, and most welcome that was as I seemed to get an enormous appetite with all the outdoor work I was doing. I remember little Mrs Church in Langham Road who never failed to remind me to "shut the gate" on my way out to prevent her little toddler Pauline from straying into the road. I met so many people then who are still my friends today, like Phyl. Her husband was away in the army and she herself was working at the local railway station and quite often due to her shift work she was at home when I delivered the milk to her mother, and we would stand at the door chatting.

One of the highlights of my morning routine was meeting up with other milk girls also doing their daily milk rounds and we couldn't pass by without a brief chat if we had time.

There was Ella who drove round majestically like a modern Boadicea with her horse and cart that she managed so well, particularly her U-turns in the main road. I didn't envy her mode of transport, I could never have coped with a horse as well as she did and it must have been so cold in the winter.

The rest of us drove vans varying from the reasonably smart to the downright ramshackle, and the worst of all, I think, was the green van that Joan drove. She and I used to meet daily in Brightling Road near the cricket bat factory where I had four customers and she just one. Poor Joan, she took her life in her hands every morning when she set out in that decrepit vehicle; for a start it had no brakes, at least not so that you'd notice! Her mode of stopping was to use a brick with a piece of string round it and she would open the van door, leap out with the brick and place it quickly and strategically in front of a wheel and hopefully this would bring the van to a halt. To start off again she just pulled the string, shoved the brick inside at the ready to be pushed out at the next stop. It sounds hilarious now, though it must have been anything but funny at the time, especially on one of the rather steep hills she had to go down past some nearby soldiers and they, knowing the situation of Joan and her van would suddenly leap out in front of her making the poor girl move even quicker with her brick for fear she might leave the road littered with run-over soldiers. It might have taught them a lesson if she had hit them. Thank goodness for Joan's sense of humour which she really needed the day she had to exchange her van for a horse and cart and was coming down what is now Knelle Road and which was then a badly rutted unmade up road, when the horse bolted and Joan, clinging on for dear life, milk cans rattling like mad things, managed to turn the horse down into Brightling Road, but nothing would stop it and as they careered on, poor Joan was almost afraid to look in case the level crossing gates were shut. Horse, cart and Joan charged along as though they were part of the Ben Hur chariot race. Thank goodness the gates were open and it was a very thankful milk girl that finally got her horse under control just before she hit the High Street and the traffic.

Back at the farm where she worked, things didn't always go smoothly for Joan and washing the cows ready for milking one afternoon she finished one half and started busily on the next when she was stopped just in time from giving the bull a good wash, something he might not have appreciated one little bit.'

Ann Bibbings highlights one of the recurring problems:

'The farm I was sent to, along with a girl named Gladys, was owned by two bachelor brothers, one of whom had been engaged for 20 years. As you might guess, two young sweet girls landing on a farm like that had its problems, the one who had been engaged thought he'd like a change so we had to enlighten him "nothing doing".

Elsie Druce leaves us with an unforgettable picture:

'Mr Robson was always a bit too keen to get cosy with his land girls and even though he had a wooden leg he could move pretty fast and get up a good turn of speed round the barn. I found the best way to deal with this was to get a long way ahead then call out, "Mrs Robson, could you come out please, for a minute".

10

OUR SOCIAL LIFE

It is true that here again there was a great divide between those girls who worked alone or lived in billets and those in hostels. Those of us living far from civilisation relied a great deal on determination and ingenuity to have any sort of social life at all, though sometimes we were just too darned tired!

Eva Briley told me that on her first farm she went out to a dance, a two-mile walk, and the farmer said she must be back by 10 p.m. At the dance Eva forgot the time, no magic pumpkin appeared and, true to his word, the farmer removed the key and refused to open the door—she spent the night in a haystack!

Sometimes nearby villages sported a hall for dancing and Zelah Skinner remembers:

'The sixpenny hops in the village hall were well attended. It was often the shy local lads who were wallflowers and we either had to ask them to dance or dance female with female, sometimes we went to a "hop" in the next village or to a large house the army had taken over, which had a grand hall. For the cinema it was a trip to Ashford, or perhaps ENSA concerts.'

Doris Rowland found getting to the dance was not plain sailing:

'I can remember whilst staying at one billet, going out to collect my only pair of silk stockings from the clothes line, prior to going to a dance, only to find just the tops hanging there. A calf had made a meal of the rest; I was not amused!'

Theo Rice's amusements, however, took another form:

'The farm land bordered Kitchener's Estate, taken over by the Tank Corps. Quite often we were invited to Lady Broome's residence for musical evenings. Bette was an excellent pianist, Wilfred Pickles's cousin (a member of the Tank Corps) played the violin and another the cello. My contribution was to turn the pages of the musical score.'

Then of course there was the cinema, or rather a film show in a local hall. Betty Jackson and her two friends went to enormous lengths to get there:

'The last bus would leave Bishops Stortford at 9 p.m. and that would mean missing the last part of the film. The three of us, June, Micky and I decided to take the milk float with Kitty the float pony in the shafts. Permission was given by the farmer and the rest was left to us. There was a Romany family on the Green, the husband did casual work for the farmer, he was so handsome with his trilby worn at an angle and his red knotted scarf worn round his neck, we girls named him Mexican Joe. He lent us a pair of beautiful coach lamps for the sides of the float. For the rear light Micky sat at the back holding my rear bicycle lamp. I took the reins and June was beside me. What I wasn't prepared for was Kitty to stop at every house that I delivered milk to and just would not budge until I got down and pretended to deliver milk!'

Joan Law tells of tremendous efforts to get to a dance, for which tickets had already been bought costing 2/6d each (12½ pence), a good price then:

'We were anxious to go and we asked our boss but he said no, we had to plant a field of potatoes by hand before we could go. This field was a steep slope so no machinery could be used. A sack of seed potatoes was put at the end of each row and we had to carry enough for a row in a big bag with a strap over one shoulder. We had to drop one potato in front of each foot as we walked along. By the time we finished the groove was thick and deep cut into our shoulders. Not to be outdone we cycled home, bathed and met at the dance, where we were to sit all evening too jiggered to move.'

Brenda Penfold comments on a modern hazard:

'...the safety of walking home after the village hop, sometimes about three miles with other villagers dropping off on the way, no worries at all about being attacked. The cinema was the local army hut about two miles away, which was also fun. Dancing in Nottingham, and going to the "Goose Fair" by the River Trent.'

Enid Dalloway remembers local dances and picture shows:

'Working hours were much longer, which was perhaps just as well as there really wasn't a lot to do once work was finished and it was in the evenings that I missed home and Brighton most of all. After the busy social life we always led it seemed so dull to spend evening after evening just sitting writing letters or reading, or in the summer, going for walks. Occasionally there was a dance in the Village Institute Hall, and they had pictures there too, for which you queued for ages to sit on a hard chair to watch a film you'd probably seen in the comfort of a cinema a long while before. But I had to laugh at the way the film kept breaking down and the audience would revel in catcalls and shouting and stamping of feet. I also joined a sort of club that met weekly in the Scout Hut and we dabbled in amateur dramatics that never really materialised into anything. Still, it was all quite fun and helped to while away the time as well as being a way of making new friends.'

And what about the morning after? Doris Hall says:

'Many's the time I have turned up at a cowshed on my bike at 5.30 a.m. in a dance dress, much to the goggle-eyed cowman's amazement. I used to say, "Just had a late night!"'

Like others, Phyllis Corry joined in 'entertaining the troops' and it paid dividends:

'The village like others had socials to entertain troops and I was asked if I would sing. The girl who played the piano was a farmer's daughter and her brother took me home the night of the social and became my husband.'

The 'hostel girls' were more fortunate in that as well as having each other's company, their invitations to camp dances usually included the offer of transport. There were of course many different nationalities in army camps and Connie McNichol seems to have met them all:

'We all went dancing on Saturday nights in the Plaza at Dumfries where it always seemed to me the youth of all the world was gathered. The Headquarters of the Norwegian Army in exile was in Dumfries; there was an Advanced Flying Unit at an airfield just outside the town at which were trained units of the Free French, Polish and even a Turkish unit at one time, as well as our own Air Force; and many British Army units were billeted in mill buildings round the town.

While I was at Ken Bridge, one of my Glasgow friends who was in the WAAF was posted to Dumfries and this brought home to me the unfair treatment of land girls as compared with the other services. My friends in the WAAF were even issued with underwear, whereas out of our 18/6d per week we had to buy our own, and worst of all, we had to pay our own ordinary rail and bus fares when we went home on leave, while the others either were issued with free passes or got fares at special rates—and they could be promoted and get higher pay—there was no promotion in the Land Army!... One poor misguided soul was treated with blank astonishment when she suggested we should spend our clothing coupons and money buying curtains for our large bedroom windows at Dalarran Lodge, Ken Bridge.'

As expected the arrival of the Americans and their easy generosity made a great deal of difference to the off-duty times of those near the camps. They are remembered among other things for the food, and also for the standard of entertainment offered. Glenn Miller played at some of the dances and Enid Ballard found that on attending a USA camp dance James Cagney was there.

Irene Algie was among those often invited to camp dances:

'An invitation was sent to the warden of the hostel, who allowed those who were dancers to go. Certain nights we had to stay in, washing, ironing, writing letters etc. At the American camp dances supper was a highlight as we got the luxury of food so different from our rations.'

Kathleen Ellis and her friends were among those sometimes invited to dances held at a US camp near Oxford:

'...when the Yanks came over a lot were stationed near Oxford and we were sometimes invited to go to dances. Because of clothing coupons we hadn't many posh dresses, so we used to share. One night it was my turn to lend my "best dress" so I didn't go to the dance, and guess who the bandleader was—Glenn Miller of course.

Also near Glympton was a small Air Force station they hadn't any WAAFs so we went to the dances. We had bikes, and there we were all dressed up, scarves round our hair which had been set with sugar and water. I was friendly with a medical orderly "Doc" by name, quite innocent because by then I had married my airman, and Doc was also married. One night he said would I like to see his rabbits. A warning voice said, "No", but Doc wasn't like that, so I went, and quickly came back again. Yes, I'd been caught again.'

I. Pamphlett, too, had splendid times courtesy of the USAAF:

'There were three USAAF aerodromes around us so we had a good time as the village had a dance every week. We got a late pass for that, as other times we had to be in by 10.30 p.m. a late pass was till 12 p.m. They were very strict on time and used to shut the door and you had to ring and you lost your next late pass. At times we were able to help our friends, or they would help me by tying the sheets together and pulling them up. We could get away with it as our bedroom was round the back of the house.

The USAAF had dances at their bases which was great as they had such lovely food and plenty of ice cream. They had these big bands and we even had Glenn Miller's band.

They got up lots of things, I remember one time they asked us out on a picnic, so they came and picked us up with a flat hay cart with the hay laid on it. There were about 20 of us and they got all the drinks and food, and we danced and ate and had a lovely day.'

Doreen Leibrandt, too, mentions the quality of the US dance bands:

'We would go into the town for our time off. It had the smallest cinema that I have ever seen and we often joked that if you paid with a note the locals thought you were trying to buy the building! Unfortunately there was no dance hall in the town and this was a disappointment until the invitations from the various forces based in the area began to increase. How very good some of these dance bands were, out in the "sticks". Later on in the war we had to learn the "American Shuffle", which had nothing to do with dancing, but an awful lot to do with saying NO! Even so the tins of jam and other food were very useful in the hostels.'

Sheila Gordon-Rae compares the arrival of the Americans with a previous invasion:

'I'm sure that the arrival of the Americans, roaring through the villages in their trucks, and jiving at the "hops" was something that all land girls will remember... When you think about it, it was almost like the Roman invasion—people with a strange accent and culture and in uniform!'

Gladys Foster found there was quite a bit of social life in the hostel:

'I remember one dance we had when some bright person had the brilliant idea of putting some soap flakes on the concrete floor to try to make it more slippery. It rained; we had mounds of congealed soap stuck to the bottom of our heels.'

Quite near the hostel where Mabel Williams lived there was an army camp and at one time it had Scottish soldiers:

'When they came to the dances dressed in kilts we went in breeches, thick socks and shoes. What laughter we had. But most times the girls went to dances in pretty dresses.'

Joan Hawell found the social life at the hostel was good and the girls all got on remarkably well:

'The Royal Engineers were camped nearby. They were 853 Regiment I recall and were a Quarrying Company. They were mostly Cornishmen, who sang Cornish songs very well and also had a good band. We land girls were treated with a brotherly interest. We were allowed to use their NAAFI and were invited to their weekly film shows and anything else going. Using their band, they held dances every Friday, in the village school, which we all, and anyone else from the village, went to. We, in turn, had parties at the hostel quite frequently, inviting the REs and any RAF boyfriends. The RAF were stationed not too far away. Some of the REs built a huge fireplace in our recreation room, a wonderful improvement on the old round stoves we had. So, we were able to sit in our armchairs, partaking of the heat from the great logs that burnt in the grate. Some years ago I went back to Woodstock to find our old hostel. Sadly, it is all gone. A newly built estate stands on the site of so many memories, as if they had never been at all.'

Angela Lincoln says that back in the hostel there was lots of fun:

'We had a table tennis table, a small radio and a piano. Many of the girls could play and two were singers, one sang all the classics and the other popular ones... The Toc H at Evesham—they were the *only* people who really did a lot for us. The YWCA were very nasty to us.'

Betty Otway, too, had entertainment at the hostel:

'Entertainment was a spasmodic thing for us, we never had an ENSA visit to my knowledge, but we did have about three CMA visits and they were of a good standard with excellent musicians, pianists, singers, ballet dancers, oboeists and the like. Several times we had a man who came in to show films, he had a generator in the back of the van which never seemed to work properly for very long, so the film took ages and ages because of the frequent breakdowns... For the rest of the time we made our own entertainment, ran a few dances, put on a few plays to raise money for the benevolent fund, went in for a competition here and there which was judged by an outside adjudicator... When funds permitted we went to the local cinema—at least ten miles away so the bus fare was needed too, this was on a Saturday, the last bus back was at 9 p.m. or thereabouts.'

Chris Breeze found an attraction at the local hop where the army dance band was playing:

'We were in our uniforms and when we entered there was this soldier playing the accordion, and he gave me a wink and the glad eye! He also played the piano, it did not take him long to make my acquaintance. It was love at first sight; we met and married within four months and we have been married 46 years.

Near our digs we had the Americans stationed also the Air Force and the Army, so we really had a lot of fun. When Roy and I wanted a bit of a cuddle we would go to an old farm house which had been evacuated because it was on the firing range. One night we were there and all of a sudden there were army manoeuvres, all the soldiers came running through the cottages shouting with their guns at the ready. Lucky for us they did not come up the stairs!

Weekends when I could get home we used to take Roy's accordion case filled with food for my mother. The Americans had plenty: salmon; corned beef, jellies, dried egg. My mother was very grateful.'

Then of course there were the girls who provided amusement for others, Vi Bromley, for instance:

'There was a company of soldiers billeted just out of town and one of them had been in the theatre before the war. He suggested getting up a concert with the help of us ladies. Well he did just that, and I am not boasting when I say it was a big success. I had more laughs rehearsing, considering I had never done anything like it before, neither had any of the others. It was held in the YMCA in the church. All 40 from the hostel were there to give their support and the Army and the locals who talked about it for days. The proceeds went to the Red Cross and St John's Ambulance.'

And Jean Emerson and her colleagues were also ambitious:

'Our Warden was approached at very short notice to see if the WLA would like to be represented at an evening's production in the theatre. It was to be in the form of tableaux and representing the services who had taken part in the war effort.

A group of us arrived at a meeting in the theatre the next morning to discuss what we were going to do. We really hadn't a clue. Undaunted, as always, the WLA got its act together. The next evening we made our plans. We would have a "Goddess of Earth" and she was to be draped in a dark green bathroom curtain. A wreath of leaves around her head and a sash across her bosom, proclaiming her status. She was holding the WLA shield. Around the stage were girls with rakes and hoes, a few potato pickers with spuds and buckets, bales of straw and hay, and to complete the picture a milkmaid with stool and milking pail. And so it was, and on the night we sang two verses of *We plough the fields and scatter* helped out by a local band, and the audience loved it.'

Dorothy Fox worked in Wales and shows just how important 'socialising' was to the girls:

'...we moved to a hostel five miles from Abergavenny, where the bus service was almost non-existent... This was a very old house, lit by oil and Tilley lamps. It gradually filled up with girls from various parts of the country, quite a number from the Welsh valleys who were kind enough to take us home for weekends...

Some girls were quite devastated as there was no cinema, fish and chip shops, no dance halls... two pubs, the Red Hart and the White Swan... we had cinema shows at the hostel from time to time...

The first highlight of our lives was when the warden invited a party of wounded soldiers to our hostel to have tea with us, and they invited us back to their place and tried to teach us to play billiards and snooker—they gave up in disgust with me!'

Dorothy Fox continues describing another hostel:

'Our Warden invited a truck full of American GIs one evening to take us to a local village hall to dance, so we donned our best "bibs and tuckers" and climbed aboard, only to find the said village hall was not much larger than the average sized lounge and no way could we all have fitted in—let alone dance. We ended up at the Beaufort Arms and continued to have visits from the American boys until 751 Division moved out. Some girls continued to keep contact with the GIs and one became a GI bride, and from the photos she sent from the States, was one of the lucky ones.'

Gladys Benton remembers Americans thinking the land girls were prisoners:

'The evenings were spent either in walking down to the village pub or else in the lounge of the hostel, where we would sit around an old piano, singing. We had one girl who could play any sort of music and she was also the life and soul of the parry. Some evenings we would be taken by truck to a nearby American Air Force base. The Americans treated us well. We taught them how to ballroom dance and they enjoyed giving us lessons on how to jive. We looked forward to those evenings, not only for the music and the company, but also for the food!

The first time the Americans saw us girls working in the fields they thought we were prisoners doing time. They had never seen girls working so hard.'

Julie Gazy and her friends had to be back at the hostel at a 'reasonable' time:

'There wasn't much social life here, a small cinema, a Nissen hut to be precise, and when it rained one had a job to hear the sound track. The local church and couple of pubs one called The Woolpack and the other The Chapel—it was the latter that was always packed with Yanks and WLA. I think the proprietors must have made a bomb. But we all had to be back in the hostel by 10 p.m. or there was hell to pay from the Matron.'

Joy Enderby mentions curfew time too:

'We had social evenings at the hostel, entertaining the local RAF, Army etc. Naturally these had to finish by 11 p.m. at the latest if it was Friday evening, 10.30 p.m. during the week. A friend and myself used to cycle about four miles to the RAF fighter drome at Odiham for the weekly dance. We both had our respective partners for different dances and usually came home loaded with goodies for the rest of the girls. There were sad times of course when the particular boy friend did not return from a mission.'

Betty Ambler and her boyfriend provided music for the hostel, although her hoped-for party going didn't come off:

'My husband and I love classical music and when I was in the WLA (he was my boyfriend then) he let me take some of his records back to the hostel, and now when Pavarotti and Carreras are so popular I often wonder if the girls remember when I used to play the records of Gigli and Tauber and other tenors and they sang the same numbers as Pavarotti and Carreras are singing today. Their music used to ring through our hostel.

I remember when I was 21 my mother had arranged a party for me and she made a cake, neighbours helped with the rations and then what do you think? I had to work that weekend so everyone went to my party but me, and what was I doing? I was clearing a big field of stones and boulders so that it could be cultivated for reseeding.'

Phyllis Weston, too, had a 21st birthday party with the other girls:

'At the hostel most of the Bristol girls who were there were all 21 years old in March, so Mrs MacKinnon, the Warden, said we could have a party and invite any boyfriends... My mum made me a cake out of some fruit she had given to her and a very old friend of hers made me a 21 key out of the lid of a cardboard box and put some silver paper on it.'

Joan Waight's hostel was a few miles from an RAF station:

'...we used to get invites to dances, sometimes they would send a lorry for us, but when one was not available we would borrow the cycles and cycle along the dark lanes one behind the other, with one lamp between us hoping we would not be stopped...'

Betty Venn and her friends sound a bit like the Bisto Kids—on the outside listening in:

'We managed to enjoy leisure times. Six or eight of us would cycle to the banks of the Severn, near Tewkesbury, to the pub by the river, light a fire, Lilian would play her accordion and a good evening spent there... not much money there. We sometimes would go to a lane near the centre of Gloucester called Oxbody Lane and listen to the dance band inside the Guildhall, could not afford to go in. But in Sandhurst we would occasionally have a dance in the village hall. George Warren, the boss's son would come, 6ft 3in tall, not handsome, rather uncouth, hands like ham bones. When he danced, guess he must have thought he was pushing the cows around, but we had to be nice to him, he was not used to so many girls around him.'

Molly Andrew says she had a good social life:

'An American hospital was nearby and the walking wounded would often be outside our hostel, as it had a lovely avenue of trees and a green, which was and still is as far as I know the village cricket ground.'

But Elsie Druce takes us through the year, and tells how the hostel nearly turned into the Palm Court Hotel:

'Winter did bring snow and we sledged down the hills with the local children. Even to midnight poaching a Xmas tree for our hostel and a policeman yelling out in the darkness for us to go home or he would tell our mothers. As for entertainment, the War Agricultural Committee sent down some entertainment. Three ladies in particular got a varied reaction, one played the cello, one the violin and one the piano. They did this all the time with their eyes closed. I can still feel now how the benches we were sitting on were vibrating with suppressed giggles. Our hostel was only 100 yards from the lovely beach and we rode our bikes along the coast to Seahouses, a fishing village, where the fishermen took us over to Holy Island and past the Farne Islands... we had it to ourselves... I remember it was a hot day and in the middle of the field we thought we would take a walk to perhaps find a stream. The next fields seemed to dip away and when we got to this dip it turned out to be a valley. Once, long ago, it had been an orchard and as far as you could see was pink blossom. We stuck it in our hair, our overalls, decorated our bikes and carried loads back to the hostel.

Also I remember the station master, when we went home at the weekends, always gave us a red rose for our button holes.'

PART TWO

11

DAIRY FARMING

To the uninitiated dairy farming meant sitting on a stool beside a cow, milk flowing as if by magic into a bucket between the knees. However, we learned that udders had to be washed (how on earth did they get so dirty?), milking and dairy equipment scrubbed, milk pails hoisted to pour the milk into the cooler, records kept of the milk yield of each cow, and sometimes delivering milk nearby after the churns had been rolled outside to be collected. Food for the herd had to be grown—no, silly, grass wasn't enough! If the farm was a mixed one there were other jobs to learn about and of course at harvest time everybody joined in.

Those girls who had no training at all were in for a few shocks but some, like Violet Farrant, won through:

'I was asked if I would like to work with the dairy herd, there were about 30-40 cows and three girls. I found hand milking a bit hard at first but it was a lovely job. I loved the cows and often had to be midwife when they were in trouble. I also had seven beautiful Hereford bulls to look after. They were my pride and joy and I spent a lot of my spare evenings grooming them.'

So much, however, depended on the farmer himself, as Kathleen Ellis found out:

'We set off to our hostel which was just outside Woodstock, it was in a big park called Glympton. The hostel was a lovely big old house in the middle of the park. We were shown to our dormitory, a huge room with ten beds down either side, and we started unpacking, then down for some tea, which was thick slices of homemade bread and fresh BUTTER and jam—it was lovely. At bedtime we were told to put out our dungarees and boots for the morning. One of the cockney girls called Nell, I think, told us the way to soften our boots was to wee in them and leave them overnight, but "no way", a few of us said, how sorry we were to be! After a very uneasy night with an occasional sob here and there, we were awakened at 5 a.m.— at least six of us were. We dragged on our jumpers and dungarees and boots and staggered downstairs to a mug of hot tea. Then into the jeep to be dropped off at different farms.

I trudged up the muddy lane to the farm and knocked at the door, an evil looking old farmer opened it and his looks told all, he never spoke, just nodded his head for me to follow him into the cowshed (I thought I had joined to be a tractor driver). All the cows were there swishing their tails and mooing, I felt sick, I was afraid of cows. The farmer threw a brown coat at me and a piece of white muslin. I put the coat on but I couldn't think what to do with the muslin, the farmer pointed to my head so I presumed I had to put it over my hair. He then returned with a stool and a bucket, but first of all, without speaking, he made me understand that I must wash the udder and teats, so I did. Then I sat down on the stool and began to perform.

What a performance! I pulled and pulled at the teats but not a drop of milk could I get, the cow kept swishing her tail across my back, and then she did a great cow clap which splashed all over me. I was near to tears when one of the farm hands took pity on me and told me to pull and squeeze the teats, after a few attempts I managed to get a stream of milk, but by then the cow was so fed up it lifted its back leg and sent me flying. I just sat there and burst into tears, the kindly farm hand came and took me to another cow and I managed to get the rhythm at last.

The jeep came to fetch me back to breakfast of bacon and egg and fried bread, it was wonderful... That night about six pairs of boots stood at the bottom of six beds, with slight steam coming out of them—it did the trick!

...I liked going to the farms that had electric milkers although sometimes I had a bit of difficulty getting them on the teats, I'd get three on and just as I was putting the last one on the other three fell off.'

Maisie Geraerts, too, found the farmer initially unhelpful:

'Being a Londoner I was, to say the least, apprehensive. The farmer wasn't too helpful, he gave us a bucket and stool each and said, "Get on with it." We sat there for ages not getting any milk until he showed us what to do... We started at six in the morning after half an hour's cycle ride, until six at night.'

Joan Welbourn too, untrained, was left to get on with it:

'I was sent to a farm to live in—a dairy farm. You had to be out by 6 a.m., milking. My first attempt ended in disaster—you were not really shown what to do, just given a three-legged stool plus a bucket and left to get on with it. Yes, I did achieve half a bucket of milk and then the cow kicked out and I lost all the milk...

One day I had to go with the farmer's son to take a calf to market, maybe walk two miles—that was alright although the calf didn't think so, just go so far and wouldn't budge, and I ended up finding a wheelbarrow.'

Barbara Youngman found what so many of us did, that cows have a personality of their own, and I still have fond memories of Ladybird, a Friesian, so good tempered. Barbara's experience, however, was different:

'One cow called Belinda just hated me and I had bruises every day to prove it. Old George was very good and would "do" her for me, but one afternoon he was off sick and the 4 p.m. milking took me until 8 p.m. when my landlady panicked because I wasn't home and rang the farm... By this time I was in tears and I told the farmer Belinda had got to go, how awful she was, couldn't be milked etc. He took the stool from me and sat beside her and milked a pail of milk and the old devil chewed the cud so contentedly while he did it. I was so angry I picked the pail up and tipped it all over her head. Belinda went to market the next time and I didn't kiss her goodbye.'

Betty Schibler too found the cows were not the placid creatures we had imagined:

'The cows were not very keen on us two girls. They used to kick hard when we put on the machines and we had to be very quick at it, as they could give you a nasty injury... but we never let them get the better of us. After the milking we had to wash and sterilize all the equipment then to collect the milk and cream and butter that we had hand churned and go to the farm for breakfast (I think we had earned it!)...

The next farm was permanent and I stayed there. It was only horses for working with, no machinery or tractors. I was working with a beautiful elderly shire horse. In the morning to catch him in the field I would take a bowl of oats then take him back to the farm stable, harness him up and mix up sacks of cereal for the young calves, load up and go across the farm on the hill to feed the calves. The next field was for kale cutting, a wet and cold job in winter. My hands used to get frozen during this, then when the cart was full I would take it to the cows, and then collect the eggs usually laid in the haystack.'

Irene Poulter went into dairy farming as a land girl after the poultry farm on which she was working had to close due to difficulties in getting the feed. She is one of only five girls with 100% diploma for milking and cattle work. She enjoyed working with pigs too, although her mother was horrified when she reported that she had had to hold the pigs whilst they were castrated. May Readey was greeted with a certain amount of reserve by the farmer's wife with an admonition to desert the yard whenever the bull was brought out to serve one of the cows:

'At milking time I went out to the cowsheds and Edgar, who was the married son who managed the farm for his father, gave me a three-legged stool and a bucket and showed me how to milk a cow. I was petrified! After tea I was shown round the farmhouse and then to my bedroom. I was given a dustpan and a goose's wing and was told that that was to be used by me to keep my bedroom floor clean. To my amazement it worked. I was told I could be number three in the bath after the farmer and his wife had bathed, all I had to do was add more hot water. I declined with thanks, and so when I had a bath I had to fill the set boiler with water from the pump outside, light a fire and carry the water up a flight of stairs.

One Sunday it was very hot and Muriel and I decided to put our bathing suits on and dunk ourselves in the stone horse trough in the yard. We laughed and splashed and eventually got out and dried ourselves in the dairy, but trouble was brewing, for when the waggoner put the horses to drink the following morning they refused. I had to confess what Muriel and I had been up to and for my sins I had to empty the trough and refill it with fresh water from the pump...

One of the jobs I took on myself was to take William our Hereford bull out for water. He and I would saunter down to the pool quite amicably. I had done the job for months until one morning I let him out a little earlier than usual and as he saw the tail end of his wives going down in front of him he went berserk. I am glad to say the Gaffer rescued me and I was told not to take William out any more.'

I, too, was told to take the bull for a walk. I was sure the cowman was 'having me on' but, no, off he went. Joyce Murphy was also on the bull run:

'My friend and I used to have to take the Red Poll bull for a walk every day, and this day we were walking him down the lane when the stick that was supposed to be clipped on the ring on his nose, wasn't... but that old bull was so used to his daily walk he didn't know!'

The bulls seem to have left indelible memories, as Amy Johnstone found:

'...I was told to go and muck out this building—oh well, get on with it, when I realised I had company—there was a huge bull shut in this stall. I was supposed to muck him out? But meantime make friends with him, give him a bit of my "piece" for it was too smelly to eat a "piece". Afterwards I blessed the day I became friendly with old Charlie.

We moved from that farm to another ten miles up the road, we three girls moved all the cattle on the hoof on three days and guess what?—I got Charlie to move with a halter round his neck. Thank goodness there was no traffic on the roads then, except the odd army lorry and *that* was something!.... We settled in and I got quite good at various jobs after the blisters healed and the muscles settled into place. It was a lovely summer too, the nearest I ever came to sunstroke in the middle of a hayfield....

We were getting the herd along nicely and old Paddy (cattleman) had shouted less—he was trying to impress others working in the hayfields. We got to this field... Margaret ran to open the gate and the cows trotted in, the calves ran off and Charlie sauntered in—I said to him as he went through the gate, "You'll like it here old fella.".... I'll never know why Paddy had to follow Charlie twenty yards into the field banging away at Charlie with his stick—then it happened! Charlie just made sweep round and lifted Paddy into the air and circled to gore him where he lay on the ground.

I could only hear myself screaming to Margaret, "Go for help", as I ran towards Paddy lying prone on the ground and Charlie giving him biffs with his head. I then kept saying to Charlie, "No Charlie, no Charlie," and he backed away. I stood over Paddy and Charlie went round and round us mooing softly, while I told him he had been very bad—that was one of the longest ten minutes of my life until the gardeners came with a door and hoes to ward off Charlie, but he walked away! Poor Charlie never did get to enjoy his field of buttercups, he was put into solitary confinement.'

Weather too played an important role in our lives—no summers were so hot, no springs so wonderful, no autumns so beautiful, no winters so—well, Dorothy Harmer knew about them:

'Oh those bitter cold days at Consett, Co. Durham. I was used to the North East, having come from South Shields on the Tyne, but winter on a farm up there was something else. Like the time the water fountains froze in the cowshed and I alone had to carry buckets of water about 30 yards from the stable trough to over 30 cows, two buckets at a time and each cow drank an average 2½ buckets. Pulling swedes when the ground is frozen and your hands bleed with the cold....'

Winter time—1947—has remained in Cynthia Banbury's memory:

'... ending up in the Cotswolds near Chipping Campden, this time starting up a Gascoigne milking parlour out in the fields, no other WLA at all but other workers and a girl groom.... Cannot forget the winter of 1947, snow covered everything, including the milking parlour. We did dig it out but it took us ages to even get down to the field it was in. The farmers were away, everything froze up, no milk collection, we used as much as possible in the house and cottage, but the rest had to be poured away, not enough churns to store it in. Eventually when the roads were cleared we got the milk down a steep hill on a sledge and found the returned empty churns full of loaves of bread. By golly, we were grateful, consuming nearly half a loaf at a meal....

I carried buckets of milk on a yoke across the yard. The goats would wait, especially the Billy, sizing you up nicely, he knew just when to take off and catch up with you in the small of the back, milk slopping everywhere.'

Betty Jackson too, recalls a bad winter:

'My next farm was at Horncastle. There were five land girls, three dairy and two general farming. It was the very bad winter of 1941–42—I had never experienced weather like it, snowdrifts six feet deep, water was perpetually frozen in the toilet jug in my bedroom, toiletries were often done in the steamhouse before milking. Chickens froze on their perches and were quickly disposed of in the boiler....

Milked 50 cows between five of us twice a day. The most wonderful experience for me was Christmas morning 1941, a first time calving heifer, after a long and difficult birth produced a lovely little calf and as it was put beside her she looked round at us with her big soft eyes....

Mollie, one of the milking gang, got married New Year 1942. We all turned up at the little church in working clothes and gum boots and it was so cold the bride wore slacks under her wedding dress.'

Enid Dalloway soon settled into her new way of life:

'The day started with milking and for the first week or so I didn't have to be at work till the late hour of 7.30 a.m. when the actual milking was almost over. My job was to get it all bottled and ready for delivery as we had a daily milk round to do. Once I was used to this then I would take turns with Eileen, a local girl who also worked on the farm and who I was to become great friends with, going in early to milk the cows and Eileen coming in later to do the bottling.

In those days we had quite a selection of bottles, not just daily "pinta" but half pints, one and a half pints and quart bottles, each to be filled to the top and a silver foil cap fitted on, using a little hand machine. The one and a half pint bottles were the older pattern with wide tops and for those we used the round cardboard discs so beloved of schools for making woolly pom-poms! Then the bottles were all put in crates and while the farmer went for his breakfast I would load the crates into the van for delivery, and then clean and tidy the dairy.

The mornings I had to be in early for milking I was invited to have my breakfast at the farmhouse, something I very much enjoyed, and I remember the steaming bowls of porridge with brown sugar and thick cream, a real luxury, as it was a long time since cream had been available on general sale, but I suppose it was considered one of the perks of a dairy farmer! We certainly had good appetites after a couple of hours' work.

It was only a small farm and we milked on average about 12–14 cows which usually provided us with all the milk we needed for our milk round.... The one cow I hated milking was an enormous white one called Snowball, who was a terrible kicker. I felt quite scared of her as nearly every time I had almost finished milking her she would reward me by lifting her strong hind leg and letting fly. Sometimes the bucket went, sometimes the leg landed fair and square *in* the bucket and then she stood firm while I watched helplessly as the lovely white milk turned into a swirling mud coloured pool, and at other times the leg crashed into me and both stool and I went flying. How I hated that cow and what a relief when she was finally sold....

We weren't the only farm delivering milk and I used to meet with several other girls doing their morning rounds as all our routes overlapped, there was no zoning of milk supplies in Robertsbridge!... I soon found that the deliveries couldn't vary unless circumstances in the family changed, because of the strict rationing which varied during the war from two to two and a half hints per person, per week. Children, of course, were allowed more, as also were expectant mums, and so usually we knew before most people when a woman became pregnant as she would give us her card entitling her to extra milk. We were glad of our half pint bottles for people living alone, although how they made a half pint last two days I do not know....

When I had learned to drive the milk was still carried in a can and measured out into customers' jugs. I never could make out why these few houses didn't have bottles like the rest of our customers, but I'll never forget the morning I stopped at the first customer, opened the back door and collected the jug, carefully measured out the pint of bubbly fresh milk and then tripped on the step and dropped the lot, smashing the jug of course and for the first time realising how far a pint of milk could go, especially if it was spilt milk!

A pint of milk in those days cost fourpence halfpenny (old currency) and twopence farthing for a half pint, which seems nothing now and yet to some of my customers even the small sum took a lot of finding. I can remember one old lady who had a grown up son and daughter living at home with her and she had a half pint every day and paid for it daily as I left. Quite often she had only got twopence and would say to me, "Farden do morrow morn", which meant she would pay me twopence halfpenny the next day and without fail she always did.

She lived in a very dilapidated cottage which boasted an extremely ancient outside loo, which on one occasion made my boss beat a hasty retreat when on delivering the daily half pint, he went round the corner of the cottage to come face to face with the little old lady perched up on her loo seat, the door wide open and her little legs dangling.'

Each farm seemed to have been a law unto itself in the way it was run and Molly Campbell was one of those who found our training methods were left behind when we were out in the real world:

'The hygienic conditions applied in the cowshed during training did not apply here. On my first attempt at milking I asked the cowman if I could wash the udders.

This was unheard of. He kindly found an old piece of sacking which he dipped into a stagnant pond, and told me to get on with it. The bacteria on the rag probably did little to enhance the milk supply to the village. In any case, one of the cows was clearly tubercular, her bones sticking out alarmingly, and she was suffering from a real graveyard cough. The milk was not treated, but the villagers who brought their little cans each evening made no complaint. Finally I heard of another job and moved on without regret on either side....

I was posted to a farm near Bletchley. We three land girls arrived together to find an attractive old farmhouse, the farmer in his late 60s and, we soon discovered, a martinet.... He told us he had expected "Lancashire Mill Girls" and was rather thrown off balance when he found his expectations were not right. So instead of eating in the kitchen with the cook, which we would much have preferred, we were entertained at the Captain's table for all meals. Our 14/- board and lodging money out of our 28/- wages, certainly provided us with good food, although rather meagre for hungry girls, and a comfortable bed....

The cows were kept with fastidious cleanliness and the Captain would not have been pleased to know that after milking we used to kick the nearest cow up and milk her into our cocoa. Neither would he have been pleased to know that one of our number used to sneak across the yard after work and have a bath in the steriliser....

One day we were offered an alternative to having the afternoon off—a Saturday. We were entreated by the foreman to wash the bull's tail. Ferdinand was considered a gentle character, but locked in his pen with a bucket of Lux flakes one could be forgiven for a certain amount of apprehension. One girl was in the pen (me) and the two others stayed by the gate ready to distract Ferdie with a load of hay, should he decide to take offence. He did. Discretion as we know, being the better part of valour, the hay was offered and fortunately accepted while I and the bucket hastily withdrew. Viewed from the left his tail certainly was improved, but from the right—well, dung does stick rather.'

For those who had no training dairy farming could come as a shock as Gwen Lawrence found:

'Having never been near a cow before I was really thrown in at the deep end and very surprised to find a cow had four teats to milk!'

Gloria Lombardo too found the going rough at first:

'I was called up in 1942 and sent to Cornwall. I only had my own clothes. I was on a dairy farm and we had to milk the cows. My first one was called Carmen, she gave me a kick and then put her foot in my half-filled bucket. We were sent out some days to do muck spreading in the wind and rain and it came over our hair and faces. I was given overalls and a green jumper. We slept in a chicken run and had no mattress on our bunks. We worked hard at harvest time, on the fields at 7.30 and come off at 10.45 ready for our sleep. Some days the rain was heavy—no macs.'

Audrey Sykes was another one of those who had to learn on the job:

'Sid Usher was the cowman, a small man with a large wife and five children. They lived in a tied cottage on the farm, water from a pump by the back door, no electricity, and no indoor sanitation. The rent was five shillings a week.

The first thing was to teach me to milk. The six or so cows were kept to provide milk for the calves we reared, with a bucketful going up to the Manor every morning for the use of the family. Sid was what was known as a "wet" milker, that is, he would squirt milk onto his hands before starting to milk, hands that were none too clean to start with, and I never saw him wash the udder of a cow before milking it. That did not matter if the milk was for the calves, but the same went up to the house. As I said they were tough in those days! After two or three weeks, and two or three occasions when the cow had its foot in the bucket, I became a fairly proficient milker, and Sid was able to go on holiday, leaving me in sole charge. The poor man had not been away for over two years, as there had never been anyone to take over in his absence. My efforts were appreciated, as Mrs Goodger wrote to my mother saying how delighted they were with the way I had coped. I still have the letter.

Milking was at seven in the morning and three in the afternoon, after which the cowpen had to be cleaned, and the calves fed, some of which were only just away from their mothers and had to be taught how to drink from a bucket held in one hand, with the other over the calf's muzzle with your fingers in its mouth, and they have very sharp teeth. Altogether it was a very messy business as they would butt the bucket, as they did their mother's udder and the milk went everywhere and stale milk on dungarees SMELLS after a bit...

Sometimes the cows were close to the farm, but occasionally down the lane in one of the meadows near the creek opposite Thorney Island. During the war there was an aerodrome there used variously by Fighter and Bomber Command. It was frequently a target for German bombers and once a body was washed up from a German plane that had been shot down.'

Those of us who had to do a milk round found ourselves as unprepared as Joan Clifford:

'... started work at 6 a.m. and told I was to do a milk round in and around Banbury in the morning and farm work in the afternoon. I had a shock when told I was to drive a van, (I had never driven anything other than a bumper car at the fair!) but the farmer said they would soon teach me. My first experience of driving would have shocked the law today—the van had no brakes and no hooter, and I had to drive through Banbury Market Place on a Thursday—Market Day! I became known as the Yellow Peril. One day I had a very heated argument with a police superintendent. I had to deliver milk in the town and leave the van while I went to several customers with two large crates of milk. When I returned to the van a very large officer told me I couldn't leave the van there, so I told him that if he would carry my crates I would leave the van wherever he wanted. He eventually turned away and told me not to stay there any longer than necessary! If our money was short on a Saturday it was taken out of our meagre wages, but if it was over we never had that. I was 10/- short one week and could never find out how, but had to lose it in my wages at 5/- a week. We paid our own lodgings out of our wages.'

Margaret Bodman's laconic style gives a clear picture of her life:

'Mainly hand milking. Also chopping wood, carrying sacks of logs up lane to billet, gardening, dung spreading by hand (not exactly—we used a fork!), whitewash shed, distemper kitchen. Cutting cow cabbages, everlasting singling, watched by farmer sitting in his trap. Pulling mangels. Hedging in pouring rain with hedging hook. Stooking corn, finding a long-lost cigarette lighter in the oats months later. Hands sore with thistles. Haymaking into cocks then pitching onto wagon. Heavy work in pitch hole half way up stack. Threshing. Problems with frozen or leaking taps. Stamping down grass in silo (how times have changed now!). Cleaning the trap. The horses knew the way home from the pub but did not know which side of the road he should be on, so only just avoided him as I cycled fast down a twisty lane. Groomed horse, once broke his chain and cantered into lane. Picking fruit. A cow got into the orchard and ate so many greegages she died. Peewits, seagulls, swallows, midges and the lark—good things. Drilling seeds. Rolling using tractor for the first time—very wavy lines.

Got told off for daringly using the hay rake with the shire horse who could easily have run off with the implement and me. Watching rat catcher. Water bowls often overflowed into mangers. Cows went wild when first turned out in spring. Cows damaged garden. Bad luck to clean cowshed cobwebs. Clock in cowshed! Milked by paraffin lamps, or a torch, or candles. Watched by the boss. Dropped a wisp of hay in the yard—"don't waste it, mate". Advised "never have your back to the manger in case a cow kicks you in the stomach". Ringworm in cows. First few days, as I was new, we washed the cows' teats. Dairy out of bounds in case I saw how much milk was watered in the 17-gallon churns. A churn was dropped in loading, and milk spilled everywhere. Hand milking helped hands. Usually took 7-10 minutes to milk a cow. My record was 16 cows before breakfast. Saved Kitty from going to market with good milking and food. Cleaned cows when expecting the Inspector. A necessary output was compulsory. Cows putting their feet in the bucket, sometimes milk spilt—and me.

During air raids cows broke loose in shed, confusion. Neighbour's bull in with cattle in morning. Bull kicked me twice. Had to climb wooden ladder affixed to wall by bull's head, and avoid being poked by his horns. Chased by same bull, in the field. Bull escaped and tossed 10-gallon drums round the yard on his horns, girls terrified in the barn, I sheltered in shed till I could run for help. Bull led the herd for miles along lanes, instead of entering field gate. Put up tin by bull to stop him eating calves' bedding. Put calves in Home Guard hut. Light from shed showed in blackout.

Horse worth £100 could not be shod as another horse had fallen on the blacksmith. Large newborn calf went for us. Fingers bitten teaching calves to feed. The weather played a big part, if there was no work or it was too wet, or we were sent home ill, we were not paid. WLA lady called and said we were working too many hours so had to have a half day off per week (often 11 hours not paid).

Sometimes had to wait for weeks for my money. Supposed to have a 5/- rise in March 1943. Worked till 11 p.m. on double summer time, haymaking—awful....

Beestings and rabbits made good meals. Kittens born in copper. Jumped on mice coming out of stooks. Farm Sunday. One of the best cows, worth £50, killed by lightning. Worker ticked off for gathering sack of dandelions for his rabbits. I am small so my farmer said to my father, "When I saw her coming up the drive I thought good God what have they sent me—she's little but she's strong."

Rides in a trap along leafy lanes. Tearing along the main road on the back of a motor bike. Four punctures in my bike—vital for work. Herrings or dried egg for breakfast. Red Cross Agricultural Sale, calf fetched 50/-. Waited 1¼ hours at Food Office for ration books. WLA Benevolent Fund, trying to raise £5,000....

Second Farm.... 19 employees lined up at 5 p.m. on Fridays for wages. Always paid correctly.... I was responsible for looking after 60 head of young cattle. We had a pedigree herd of Ayrshires, which arrived at the local railway station from time to time. The herd became TT during the three years I was there, and every test proved OK and each time I was given a cash bonus! After caring for some of the calves for a few months the vet did not recognise them. I kept a careful feeding chart for each animal, week by week, so they were fed individually. I carried four small buckets of milk at a time to different calf sheds. But they always mooed as I entered the farm in the early mornings—so the sleeping farmer knew if I was late!

One of the workers would help me mix the meal (heavy work) and I helped him hand milk on a different part of the farm. One day I shook everybody by turning up in white for milking—but continued to do so with the farmer's approval. It was mostly machine milking, but some stripping. I kept the milk records and did the dairy work. It was fun to go down the fields in the evening and assess the best milker (practice for a competition). Luckily I judged correctly but one day Polly was found dead in her stall yoke. The bull went wild in the roundhouse, and I ran for help as he was attacking someone. I was not allowed in with the bull, being a woman (thank goodness).'

Frances Gregg found life on a remote farm in North Yorkshire a bleak one:

'... rising at 5.30 a.m. to milk and working through until bedtime usually. The farmer and his wife went to bed as soon as the 9 o'clock news had finished on the radio and I was expected to do likewise. After about a year of this I left and went to live in a hostel, feeling very self-conscious being surrounded by lots of other young women!'

Dorothy Brook too was in Yorkshire:

"The particular farm on which I was employed was one owned by Huddersfield Co-op Society in a remote village named Tong, situated between Leeds and Bradford. It was mainly a dairy farm with a pedigree herd of Friesian cows, registered with the Milk Marketing Board as "Hucop" herd. My work started at 6 a.m. in the morning fetching the cows in to milk—often having to walk a mile over the fields to find them—just me and my dog, no fear whatsoever of being lonely. One thing that always amazed me was how the cows always know their correct place in the mistle.

Then it was milking time and home at 9 a.m. for cooked breakfast (how I did enjoy it). Back on the farm to clear the dairy and keep all records of yield, butter fat etc., also write pedigrees out for any new calves.'

Much further south, Daphne Blanford was despatched to Chichester:

'... a properly run farm plus an excellent billet though there was a lot of disease in the herd including mastitis and contagious abortion. Hand milking was the answer which suited me as, though machine milking took over at some of the bigger farms, I always disliked it and was sure the cows responded far better to the personal touch! I very soon found a sense of humour was the answer to a great many near disasters and that once they got used to the idea of girls doing a man's job most of my male fellow workers became appreciative of our efforts, and co-operative.

Later on in the war as a respite from milking the WLA gave me a job as milk recorder, which lasted for about a year, but I then returned to milking as I discovered I missed it! Besides which, recording was very boring and involved long bicycle rides in the pitch dark mornings with no signposts to help, and I had to rise sometimes as early as 4 a.m. to get there in time.'

Jane McLaren was also sent to a dairy farm, this one with a retail business with two milk vans on the road delivering in milk to the nearby town:

'I was to drive one of the vans and deliver the milk. In those days the milk was mostly from large ten gallon cans with taps and you had to measure the milk out for each customer. Well, I started the day with my alarm clock going off at 4.45 a.m. so it was up and into the dairy to fill the milk cans etc. for the milk rounds, with some help. Then it was into the house for breakfast at 6.30 a.m. after which it was off in the van to deliver the milk. Back to the farm about 11 a.m. to write up the milk book, saying how much milk each customer had got and who paid etc.

Dinner was about midday, then it was off to do various jobs, depending on the time of year etc. When it came to 3.30 p.m. it was into the house for a cup of tea, then off to the milking. Proper high tea was after the milking about 6 p.m. The byre held about 62 cows. We had milking machines, but the cows in those days were stripped of their remaining milk by hand after the machines were taken off. There were neap baskets to fill (one for each cow) this was heavy work, as indeed a lot of it was. Then they were bedded down with straw. Of course it depended on the time of year whether the cows were in all the time, or out at night and trough the day. They had to be mucked out with a graip [an implement like a large rake] and shovel and the muck wheelbarrowed to the midden outside the byre door.

The cows got groomed and clipped at times, and course course their udders washed before milking. There would be calves to feed too, from a bucket. I had two milk laddies who helped me deliver the milk round to the customers before they went to school—and one had to keep an eye on them! The first week I was on the milk round I looked back to see if they had shut the van door and the next thing "bang, crash" I had knocked down a lamp post. I thought that would be the end of my stay at the farm, but no. In fact the story has been kept up on me to this day!

There weren't many holidays, I worked seven days a week, Christmas Day and New Year's day etc. though I did have two half days off a week. There was always the milk van to wash inside and out. How in wartime we ever saw to drive with just two slits on the headlamps amazes me now.'

Joan Hawell had, among other things, a milk delivery and found that Dolly knew best:

'I had a month with an experienced girl learning to milk. After the month I was left to help the cowman and generally help with the livestock.... After morning milking Dolly the pony was harnessed and I proudly stood in the float, with a churn of milk, and escorted her to the "Union" near the village, to deliver the churn of milk. I have said escort the pony, because she had done the journey so often she needed no guidance. As soon as the empty churn was set in the float she would set off back with me running behind and scrambling on to regain my proud position with the reins.

Charlie the cowman was a lovable little man with a great character. He had his cows to milk (hand milk), mostly the kickers, and I had mine... Mert the tractor driver impressed me by being able to roll a churn of milk with one hand.'

Marion Hinkley also had a milk round, aided (or not) by Saucy:

'I was put on another milk round for another dairy in Sevenoaks, a land girl among all men, this time with a horse and large milk float. The horse had to be caught, fed, groomed and harnessed before I trundled off round the Bat and Ball and Gasworks area. My horse, Saucy, was extremely slow. My billets were with a strict Baptist brother and sister who gave me a milk pudding of some sort every day! Social life was nil!'

There was a pony named Topsy with whom Joyce Sherman had adventures:

'My main duty was to deliver milk (bottled) to the town of Leominster, and one outlying area, in the morning and do dairy duties in the afternoon. My morning round conveyance was a cart pulled by a lovely pony called Topsy who knew her topography well, and in particular the position of the baker's shop. Her blackmailing tactics were—a sugar bun or else!

One chilling reminder of that milk round is of the morning at the depot, where I collected a second load of filled crates and gave Topsy a drink and a breather. It was a January morning, and in reaching down to the brook that ran through the depot to fill Topsy's water bucket I slipped on the ice and fell into the water getting thoroughly soaked. During the drive back to the farm, about 3½ miles, my garments froze on me. A bit more than a stiff upper lip.

The American forces stationed in Leominster called me Boadicea and often serenaded me with a popular song of the time that began "Milkman (maid), keep those bottles quiet".'

To quote Myra Hobden 'we really found out what work was all about':

'We milked 24 cows each day by hand, looked after the dairy and worked out in the fields The farmer was quite old so didn't do an awful lot himself. We were at work at 5 a.m. and finished about 5.30 p.m. in the winter. In the summer we worked until dusk. We were so tired some weeks we just worked and fell into bed as soon after our evening meal as possible....

Our hours were long and we were expected to keep up with the men. There was very little machinery in those days, at hay-making time all the hay was made by hand. Edna and I used horses to turn the hay and row it up, and then it was manhandled onto waggons and taken to the farmyard where it was made into haystacks.... We were part of a team, perhaps eight or nine men...

I moved to another dairy farm—what a difference! The farmer and his wife were so kind, they worked on the farm themselves. There was a lot more machinery there, all the milking was done by machine and we had a modern dairy.... The farmer and his wife remained our friends until they both died.'

Pam Crellin had a horror story—one that should never have happened:

'... joined the WLA aged 17½ and weighing 7 stone 2lb. After a medical by appointed WLA doctor I was sent a uniform and a rail warrant to a farm in Westmorland (nearest town Kendal). The WLA told me I would be met at the village station of Oxenhome after the day's journey from London. No one there to meet me! After setting out to walk and finding my way, a kindly local gave me a lift to a point near the farm.

Had barely arrived when the farmer took me up to the fells to see the sheep flock. Showed me how to treat the sheep foot rot (crawling with maggots) with a black ointment. The WLA said I would spend about four weeks training on the farm, learning to milk and all other skills.

There was a dairy herd of 72 cows—own bull kept—dozens of calves and heifers and bullocks to cope with. The farmer was inclined to be lazy and left most of the work to a middle-aged farm hand and myself. The WLA representative very occasionally called, and briefly at that, to see if I was surviving! I'm not sure I even knew her name or where I could contact her. No back up or support at all that I recall. I was totally at the mercy of the farmer. I worked from 5 a.m. until late in the evening. In summer until 10.30–11 p.m. Eventually the WLA did supply me with a bicycle which meant I could go into Kendal occasionally.

Eventually after about 1½ years I became ill and had a terrible cough. But carried on working. It was coming up to Christmas and the WLA rep *did* call in. She was well aware I was ill and said that as I was going home for a couple of days I would soon recover. In fact I arrived home in a state of collapse and my mother sent for a doctor—he diagnosed a form of pleurisy.

I cannot remember how long I was home ill. But when fitter the doctor said I should not be sent back to the north, and he wrote to WLA requesting I get a posting to the south. WLA replied that I was in the "services" and would go where they sent me. They enclosed a rail warrant to a farm a couple of miles away from the one I'd refused to go back to! My parents and doctor put up a fight re my health and I eventually received a rail warrant to a farm in Wiltshire. A lovely farm—at last! The farm labourer on my first farm continued to write to me and said that the WLA girl who replaced me ruptured her stomach mucking out and pushing the heavy loads by wheelbarrow. The farmer was finally refused any more land girls. At last the WLA took notice.

The farm in Wiltshire was a joy but I cannot ever remember seeing or hearing from a WLA rep during my time there. I was the only WLA girl in the village. I'm not sure where I would have turned to if there *had* been problems. Happily, there were none. My left lung was scarred and I had yearly checkups until a couple of years ago.'

Joy Morgan had training for milking and mentions a common hazard:

'My first job after training was in Gloucester on a dairy farm and I delivered the milk with a pony and cart around the town. In those days people were very shocked because I wore short shorts! I worked usually a six day week approximately 12 hours a day, sometimes 14, and this was the norm for most of my time in the Land Army.

I was frequently kicked and squashed by cows and chased by many a bull and not only the fourlegged kind. Many a farmer thought their dreams had come true when my friend and I turned up. We soon put them right on this score.'

For Joy Lawrence the 'hazard' had a happy ending:

'I moved to a nearby farm to live in as part of the family, I was told I'd taken over from their eldest son who had to join the army. His Transport Unit was passing through Canterbury so he got a few hours leave to come home to inspect the land girl. We were married a year later and I left when our first child was expected. The girl who took my place married the second son and Mr Lawrence used to say, "I had two good girls until you boys came and took them".'

Daphne Stone has memories of different personalities—were there really more 'lady farmers' then than now?

'I had been spoken for by a neighbouring lady farmer who had a herd of pedigree TT Guernseys and needed a trainee milkmaid besides help with pigs and poultry at her farm in the valley. It wasn't just the thought of the cows but the farmer herself, a French-Canadian doctor's daughter who had left a comfortable home and promising career in Quebec to come to Swanley in Kent for a course in agriculture and fruit growing in order to help the "old country" in her hour of need.

My first glimpse of her had been of what I thought was a Chinese coolie, with a hand cultivator going to and fro across the field—a moon-shaped face, almond eyes and long black hair in a bun—but she later confided to me that she had Eskimo origins, her great-grandfather having been a whaler. She was a highly efficient and fearless farmer though a most unlikely one, being steeped in English and French classics which lined the walls of her library in the Elizabethan farmhouse, and having a sister currently appearing with the Shakespeare Company at the Old Vic. The sister would occasionally visit with small daughter and Chinese nanny, so the locals were quite certain there was funny business afoot with "them furriners". To add to the fun, we had an Australian housekeeper who disliked Canadians, so very often there would be a pitched battle with cups and saucers flying in all directions. Needless to say, we met with stiff opposition amounting to hostility when we attended the market, being the only women present.

The cows being TT a strict routine amounting to a religious rite was observed before milking for both ourselves and the cows. We wore white overalls and caps into which every wisp of hair had to be pushed, and after scrubbing, hands were required to draw off and discard the foremilk of our charges. I was a slow, timid starter at milking as the teats of the newly calved Guernseys were extremely thick and "bags" seemed filled with cement rather than milk. Most nights I would shed a tear of despair that I would ever make a milker, though my fear of cows had been overcome, and I came to love them dearly from that time on.

There was also butter-making to learn (before the Minister of Agriculture clamped down on its production for retail), and care of the pigs. In those days, the sows and their families had wooden houses with spacious "runs" and the cruel "dry sow stall" had yet to be introduced.

As we were finding it increasingly difficult to get our "choosey" heifers down the lane to the Guernsey bull (one or two of them had got out and disgraced themselves with an old Shorthorn) it was decided to rear our own, and the next little bull calf to be born was to be reserved and reared as our own "stud". He arrived at midnight on my birthday and was duly registered in the Guernsey Herd Book as "Rose Lad of Pemsey". As he increased in size he became our champion, seeing off every other male in sight, especially the unsuspecting troops seeking to use our fields for manoeuvres.

By now a qualified milker, I was moved to a large mixed farm on the main road at Barrow Hill, Sellindge, backing on to the Westernhanger Racecourse. The motley herd of 25 cows were in direct contrast to the ladylike Guernseys I had been used to, and hygiene at milking time was reduced to a bare minimum, with the cowman and his son in grubby shirts and waistcoats, caps, and sometimes with a well-chewed cigarette stuck behind an ear. Although the cows were washed down before milking, and our hands were presumably clean, I was horrified when the cowman, trying to be helpful, suggested that I might find it easier if I spat on my hands before getting to work on "them tough ole speens" (the Kentish version of "teats" or "tits"). You can imagine how *they* felt when I appeared for my first milking, clad in my surgical "Pemsey" kit!'

Tibby Killick can smile at her memories now:

'I was cleaning out the byre and running the barrow-load of muck up the plank where the manure was being collected. I was well up the plank with my back to the farmyard when they decided to kill a pig. Oh the squealing was awful and down I went into the mire. Well you can guess the mess and smell.... In the morning the hens were out in the field. When I went to feed them I found the heads and feathers, it was made to look like the dear old fox, only it was two-legged ones from the army camp farther down the road. The police followed the trail of feathers from the henhouses down the road right into the camp.'

Helen Sheppard was fourth cowman on a farm near Canterbury, with 100-plus Friesians:

'I lived with the farmer and his wife and started at 5 a.m. each morning and finished about 5 p.m. I did a milk round in the village with horse and cart and churns, people leaving jugs on their doorsteps. Oh, Edwina Currie! My boss complained that I did not "socialise" with the family in the evenings to play rummy, bridge and in the summer, croquet. But I was so darned tired, I couldn't keep awake!

At another farm I was expected to raise calves for veal but after the first batch I couldn't face seeing their beautiful but accusing eyes, gave in my notice, but the farmer said, "We'll give up rearing calves", so I stayed.'

Ailsa Tanner gives a graphic description of her life, fortunately with an interpretation of 'shawing neaps'.

'My main work was with the dairy cows which were hand milked. There were about thirty milking at any one time, and the milkers were the boss and his wife, and two other girls and myself. We sat on milking stools with a metal luggie between our knees, and we had to tie the legs together of difficult cows, and tie down their dirty tails which they liked to swish into our faces. They liked to be sung to, and my repertoire of current pop songs and sentimental ballads increased greatly. As I grew more expert I could milk about five or six cows with the rest of them. Other jobs were mucking out the byre and feeding the cows, washing the milk cans and luggies and also work in the fields.

One of my first jobs in the autumn before the ploughing, was to cart dung from the midden onto the field with Peter the ploughman. He looked after the horses, lovely Clydesdales, so willing and gentle, but you can hardly see any today.

We were set to cart dung to the Ardlamont field. I was working with Pete and the other two were spreading. It was a showery day, and a day of rainbows made exclusively it seemed for Point. Walking out to the field once in the middle of a shower I seemed to be walking under an immense coloured arch with one pedestal in the dung heap and the other in the potato field... About 10.30 the Blenheim that seemed to have taken a proprietary interest in Point visited us. It flew straight over our heads many times and we could see the pilots quite plainly in the glass cockpit and they were waving away. We replied with our graips.

Regularly we threshed corn in the barn, with an engine in this case for the mill, but with a waterwheel on another farm. Here our job was to feed the mill with the sheaves and to make bundles of straw, which were on that farm called battels, which were given between two cows in the evening.

After the spreading of the dung for Peter to plough in, the winter work consisted of shawing neaps—topping and tailing the turnips with a sharp knife. This could be very hard work if it had been frosty.'

Barbara Fowler shows the sad side of farming when she tells of an outbreak of foot and mouth disease and the aftermath:

'My first job after doing my training was at Church Farm near Havant. Here I lodged with the head cowman and his rather dour Yorkshire family. I remember being permanently hungry and a friend used to send me fruit cakes which were like gold in those days of rationing. Milking started at 5 a.m. and the farm was about a ten minute bike ride away. I was woken up every morning about 4.30 a.m. with a bang on my door and a lighted candle outside it. There were no mod cons in those lodgings! Bedtime was at nine sharp and reading in bed was frowned on as candles were in short supply.

The very large Ayrshire herd was milked by machines and I was soon in charge of three of them up the very long cowshed and down the other side. There were no milking parlours in those days. Sometimes the udders were so low it was a struggle to get the machines on and just when you thought you had succeeded they would fall off and have to be washed all over again. When the milking was over that first morning I was told to go and open the gate at the top of the field to let the cows into the kale. Imagine my horror when about 70 Ayrshires with very long horns came charging up the field after me. I didn't realise they were not a bit interested in me, but just wanted to get through the gate to start feeding. I suspect there were several young farm hands having a good laugh at my expense down at the farm.

While working at Gosden Hill Farm near Guildford, there was a very bad outbreak of foot and mouth disease in the district. The farmer that I worked for had about five farms in the area, but fortunately only the one that I worked on and the calf rearing unit were infected. I well remember the morning that we waited for the vet to come after morning milking, all thoughts of breakfast forgotten. The suspect cow was standing uneasily in her stall moving from side to side on her blistered hooves with a frothing mouth. Then another wait as the Ministry vet had to confirm it. It was a sad sight seeing the blown up bodies of the cows I had grown to love waiting to be buried in the big lime pits that were dug for them. The farm dog, Blackie, was also put down. All our clothes had to be fumigated and great care had to be taken not to spread it to any of the other farms.

Many years' work was wiped out with the loss of all the calves and young stock.'

Listening to Doris Hall's stories of milk deliveries, the wonder was that those bottles ever reached their destination:

'The farm manager appeared on my doorstep one morning. He said, "The milk girl is ill and as you have driven the tractor, you'll have no trouble with the van. You'll have to deliver 60 gallons of milk every day starting tomorrow, until she is well again. I'll take you round the village in the van this evening to get you used to the controls." I started at 6 a.m., no co-driver, to deliver this milk. As you can guess I just crawled along, never having driven before. Every time I saw a bus or army lorry approaching I stopped dead. To make matters worse, I just had a book of addresses and amounts of milk. It was 9 p.m. when a search party arrived to see what had happened, and I had just finished the delivery. I did this for a week, with shorter and shorter times for delivery.

Then there was the time during 1943/44 when, working for a dairy, I delivered milk, meat, papers, groceries (milkmen had prior claims to petrol), to people in the Chilterns. I was in a very battered Austin-7 and the handbrake was useless, foot-brake not much better. When I wanted to stop I drove into the bank. It was quite a hair raising experience coming down the steep hills.

I was posted to a village called Milton Common in Oxfordshire, where I carried out the duties of a milk recorder, cycling 250 miles a week. I had to be at a certain farm at, say, 4.30 a.m to oversee the morning milking, prepare butterfat tests from the individual cows ready to be transported to Reading for testing. Go home, have breakfast, a snooze, ready for p.m. milking at another farm, I had a rota for six farms to manage. In the evenings I did my paperwork which consisted of adding the total yields of each cow and obtaining a percentage. The records then had to be sent off to Reading. This method was under the Government's TT scheme.'

Phyllis Westaway had to overcome her fear of cows, though this sounds like throwing a non-swimmer into deep water:

'... it didn't help when the first job they gave me was to groom the Hereford bull—at least he was tied up. The son, Ted, was very kind and helped me a lot, showing me how to wash the cows and then putting the machines on and then stripping the last of the milk. I got to know the cows I didn't mind doing, and the ones I avoided. The milk had to be carried up the road to the cooling plant near the house. We used a yoke and two buckets so we had to keep fit.... I learnt to harness the horse and cart and drive it with large churns of water to the poultry in the fields.'

C. B. Davenage, at 17, also went in at the deep end but fortunately had a splendid local representative:

'My next farm was a nightmare. The farmer was a bachelor with a monster for a mother! As I was only 17 (how different it is now!) they insisted on being *in loco parentis*. I worked very hard, but it was never enough for him. I had to be in bed by 10 p.m., he used to get me up in the morning by banging on the ceiling with a broom. I daren't be late or I heard about it all day. I was not allowed to get friendly with another land girl in the village as she lodged in a council house. The only reading material downstairs was *The Farmers' Weekly*, the only radio programmes were *Farming* and *The Fat Stock Prices*. I have only memories of being lonely and cold as it was November, with nothing but hard work in my life. I stood it for three weeks then fortunately our local representative, the Hon. Mrs W.R.S. Bathurst, came round checking up and it was decided I couldn't stay there....

At the next farm the farmer's wife was very generous, when we went home, often with joints of pork, after a pig had been killed, quite illegally, of course, at dead of night behind closed doors! She gave us butter and eggs and other things which were warmly welcomed by my very rationed family.

A horror story of a different sort from Brenda Golden:

'I was posted to Cuckoo Farm, West Clandon. The farmer was also tenant to six other farms in the area and later added a seventh. I was only the second land girl he employed, although by the time I left in 1945 there were about 14 working for him as well as several Italian prisoners of war from the camp on Merrow Downs.... Nearly all the farms had herds of cows. They were all Shorthorns with one herd of Guernseys. It was the cowman at Cuckoo Farm who taught me to milk properly.... Our milk was picked up each morning by lorry. The churns came in three sizes, 10, 12 and 17 gallons each, the last one weighing in at 2¼ cwt when full and needing two people to swing them up onto the ramp for collection.

The bull pens were usually filthy and merely had extra straw thrown in and were cleared out only twice a year. Fields away from public gaze were often very weedy and fag hooks were needed to cut the weeds, as hoes were totally inadequate for the job. Everything that could be done on the cheap was done that way. He was a very mean man and made a lot of money. Fresh cows were bought usually from Guildford market. He sent his rough cows to Guildford and obviously all the other farmers did the same. Some were devils to milk, some kicked, others had TB in its early stages. Some of our cows certainly had TB but were kept as long as they gave a lot of milk. Some had brucellosis and always aborted so went back to the knackerman if he couldn't get them in calf again, and sent them back to market for some other unwary farmer to buy. I'm sure our boss was not the only one who farmed like that. Regulations were not so strict and there was nobody to keep a check on everything.'

How very quickly once we became acclimatised did we speak of 'my' cows, 'my' farm and, in K. Golder's case, 'my' horse.

'... I went to dairy work delivering milk. I had a pony and float and had a lovely round meeting people, also collecting the milk from the farm. My boss was wonderful. I had to get up at 4 a.m. to be at the dairy by 5 a.m. to get my float loaded up, all weathers, and every day, also to get my horse ready. Once a week I had to clean the float and all the harness etc. I had to groom my horse every morning after delivering—I really enjoyed it. My horse often used to get me into trouble while I was delivering milk. He used to eat people's hedges in their front gardens. A lady gave him a lump of sugar and after that he would not wait for me to come along, he used to walk up the road and knock on the door with his head. I worked on my wedding day to get the milk delivered.'

May Love was sent to a farm in Wigtownshire and was there for four years:

'I was seven stone something at that time and on my first leave my mother was quite horrified that I had developed muscles—I had put on a stone.... I learnt to work in the fields at ploughing (by horse), sowing, harrowing and of course, milking.... Most of my memories are happy ones. Like singing while milking—the cows loved it! Being chased by a heifer into a stream and later finding out it had been petted by a previous land girl and only wanted to play!'

Phyllis Corry was one of those who milked and also did general farming:

'The rest of the time I was on the farm using horse-drawn implements. I can remember one morning I was nettle cutting when a patrol of soldiers came through the grounds, and one of them left the ranks to come and speak to me. The following day or so I had a letter addressed to Miss Land Girl, which I still have. The farm was hilly so a valley was formed between two farms which I believe allowed voices to be echoed.... One morning I was singing while muck spreading when a farm worker across the valley joined in. I never heard whether the villagers heard us or not!

Whilst farming itself was different from that of today, some forms of farm ownership too were different. Some hospitals had their own farms to provide milk and vegetables, the National Coal Board too owned farms.

Combine harvesters were rare indeed and the horse still ruled on many farms. When travelling around the countryside now the fields seem empty, perhaps sometimes just a tractor showing a sign of life. At harvest time there are no stooks standing ready for collection, just those huge plastic covered rolls—hence no hay ricks.

Marjorie Beasley comments on some of the changes:

'I was transferred to a larger mixed farm in Lacock, Wiltshire. Even at this time, 1945, the farm was completely behind the times. All work was done by horses and I was expected to work with these for dung carting etc. Milking was by hand, 60 cows of a very mixed bunch in a partially open very long shed. During the winter months with rain and snow we were often completely drenched two or three times a day. Time off was half a day per week and even then this was resented by the rest of the all-male staff.'

Freda Kerley too compares yesterday with today:

'I was very lucky to have a job on the farm near where I lived so I never had any worries about having somewhere to live. When I started it was hand milking—I expect it was 60-70 cows.... Helping with the harvest, there were no combine harvesters those days. We had to put the sheaves of corn into a stack, eight to a stack, and winter time we ground the mangels, mixed with meal and chaff for the cows to eat while they were being milked. Better fed those days, no mad cow disease.'

Mary Hall's experience shows how clean milk was achieved on 'her' farm:

'During the winter our cattle were housed in an enormous covered-in foldyard, so every day clean straw had to be put down, the hay ricks filled and mountains (or at least it seemed like mountains) of roots (swedes, mangels etc.) cut up and fed to the animals. Our milking parlour was used just for milking unlike most of the other farms where cattle were kept in one place where they slept, were fed and milked, consequently we produced the cleanest milk in the area.'

Like so many of us, I. Jeffrey managed to see the humour in her situation:

'After a month's training I went to a private farm to be the milkmaid. It was so funny as I was living in at the farm, and the farmer was a little man, and his wife was much taller and bigger than he was, and she certainly was the boss. He never answered her back and he used to do everything she said but when he was out on the farm he was a right boss, he used to go for me if I did anything wrong.'

Joyce Porter, however, found that enough was enough—some girls really were 'put upon':

'... sent to Greatwood near Lyneham; smallish farm run by Joe Mapson and sister Lucy. 25 cows and three bulls, milking, silage, muck spreading, ditching. Miles from anywhere. Joe and sister Lucy used to disappear more often than not, leaving my friend and myself to get on with it. Got fed up with this situation so asked for a transfer. Left after a row with Mapson, and he refused to pay us. He wasn't allowed land girls after that.'

Mary Vickery had experience of two vastly different farms:

'Having been brought up to a fairly regular routine and meal time at regular hours, I found it extremely difficult to cope with meals at any old time. Milking also was not done at set times, and I have been milking (by hand) at 10 and 11 o'clock at night....

When I left that farm I went to work for a lady farmer with a pedigree herd of Ayrshires. This farm was everything the first one was not and I had a very enjoyable three years there until I got married. The lady farmer (a spinster) was quite a character and we were very fond of her. Her cows were her family, and as I did her books and records she would walk with me and tell me the history of them. She died whilst I was there and we were devastated. She left her farm and cattle to the Agricultural Research Council who promptly sold it up.'

M. Griffin demonstrates the influence of just one man on the herd:

'We had a very cruel cowman one place I was at. The cows were afraid to move in case they had a stick on them. We had to keep very quiet all through milking, any noise they would jump and kick out and then they were hit again, bucket went flying. Most places work started 5.30 a.m., getting cows in for 6 a.m. milking. We had torches one place and a very large herd. We could hear the cows running down the fields when we called, just hoped they would not knock us flying.'

Joan Coulson transferred to milking and:

'... learned to hand milk cows with dropped udders. Besides milking I fed calves and did milk recording. As the NCB owned all the farms in this area, I sometimes covered for staff on their days off on other farms—all within cycling distance. Byremen's wives always made me very welcome at break time, with home-made scones and cakes. I also took a correspondence course in dairy husbandry. At local agricultural shows I often had to lead a cow around the ring in the final parade.'

Pat Warren's first job came as a surprise, as a milk girl on a man's cycle:

'... a push bike with some 20 gallons of loose and bottled milk can be very cumbersome, especially on a 3-mile route from Martlesham through to Woodbridge. On a frosty morning the tyres skidded and the entire contents of loose milk and broken bottles were a sight to see. Since this happened very early and in the dark I was the only witness but I had to face irate customers, some of whom hoped to have their extra ¼ pint to make a milk pudding. I grew up very quickly!'

After the horror stories, here's Elizabeth Venner who found her niche:

'I was then sent to work for Philip Nicholson, a Sheffield business man who owned a farm at Sutton Scarsdale, Mansfield. I had lodgings near the farm, and I worked with a herd of Jersey cows, milked by hand, dairy work and general farm work when I had finished grooming the cows every day. This was a very pleasant job, I was there until 1945 and the war had ended.'

Pauline Grant, writing from Virginia, was one of those who left the WLA because of injury:

'In 1943 I hurt my arm when helping with the harvesting and had to have it in plaster for six weeks. At the end of that time, the hospital put it in plaster again and suggested I find some other line of work. I do remember coming home on the train, carrying my milking stool which the farmer gave me, and enduring quite a few wisecracks from servicemen in the carriage—"must have been a tough cow" etc.

I was sorry to leave as by then I was quite adept at milking (naturally), muck spreading, dealing with chickens, shovelling coal onto a cart at the local railway station—quite a few skills which unfortunately I have not been able to use since.'

12

GENERAL FARMING

General Farming was the name given by the WLA officials to something one could volunteer for which wasn't market gardening or cows. Farms and tasks were varied (as were the farmers!). Betty Venn gives a picture of work by seasons:

'Four other girls joined us, two from Bristol and two from Yorkshire, for the arable side of farming. We all got on well, working in all weathers outside. The sugar beeting was very hard, being gathered around December/January. We stuffed our wellies with hay to keep our feet warm. We did have outside help, army, Italians, Canadians, which helped us immensely, being all young girls, which made us look forward to going to work. Lots of teasing from the boss. Come spring, more jobs to be learned, ditching and hedging and we took it all in our stride, a very hard job. Then seed sowing, muck spreading, kept us warm on a cold day.

Then we were asked to creosote all the gates and fences, and to use the drum of creosote in the outhouse. So off we went, six of us, we wondered on getting splashed why it burned. Next day the boss asked us which drum we used. There were two identical drums, but one contained sheep dip, which was very expensive, the boss was not amused. Come summer, haymaking, very long days, sometimes working in the moonlight, but a good spirit. One backslider was a farm labourer called Tom, a peeping one too, could always tell us where we had been courting. He spent most of his time rolling cigarettes, his pet job was taking the cow to the bull, no comment there.

Through spring and into the hoeing of crops, we would work overtime with pay, but very poor, but we all worked side by side on the rows, having one girl that told jokes all the while, Roma was her name.

One comment, my boss on the farm in Gloucester although bankrupt at the start of the war, became Chairman of the War Agricultural Committee, and was the richest man in the village at the end of the war, I suppose because of cheap labour.'

Joan Howell was stationed in a hostel at Woodstock from where the land girls travelled by lorry many miles to work:

'The very first day at work on a farm will be forever a memory of shame. A gang of 14 had been sent to paddle the weeds out of young corn. Imagine us all, straight from the "Big City", clad in stiff dungarees and, equally stiff, black boots with no bend in them, being given a paddle (a straight kind of hoe) to chop weeds out. We hardly knew weeds from corn.

No one came near us all day in a field that must have been about ten acres. Our sandwiches had become stale and the milk seemed to have gone sour in our flask of tea. We had left them in the sun. In the whole eight hours we had hardly covered a patch any larger than a parish room. What relief when the lorry arrived to return us to the hostel. Complaints from the farmer must have been made, as next day we were split up.'

Elizabeth Hanmer paints a winter picture—anyone who had picked frozen Brussels sprouts, or frozen anything else, will have a fellow feeling:

'The worst job was thinning turnips. About ten of us, one drill behind each other in a row, hoeing backwards and forwards interminably, day after laborious day, the men telling stories and jokes all the while. It was so boring after using your brain at school, and now this tedious, and to begin with, rather tiring job. The men were always so far ahead, being skilful at their job, and they seldom came back to help us....

Lifting potatoes became the worst torture so far. The boss marked out our "bits" to be lifted and the tractor and digger drove relentlessly up and down and masses of potatoes were scattered out across three or four feet. These we gathered into woven wicker baskets and old Geordie with his horse and cart would empty them for us. What unbelievably back-breaking toil! Within two days, the muscles on the backs of our thighs were so pulled and stretched with this unaccustomed work, we could hardly walk home, and when there, if anything fell on the floor, it remained there for days or until we could not do without it, and we'd argue for ages about who would pick it up!

Late in November I was directed to another farm... a 35-acre field of turnips frozen into the ground. To top and tail frozen turnips is a job I would never master and certainly never learn to enjoy. Each day was the same. All alone in this huge field. One morning the "hench" or turnip knife skidded off the brick-hard swede and neatly peeled the surface skin off the back of my left hand. Being cold it was extremely painful and I was feeling very sorry for myself.... About midmorning a car drew up at the end of my drill on the roadside. A nice looking old gentleman opened his window and shouted, "Come doon here a minute, lass." He asked all sorts of questions. "Are you in this huge field all on your own? Do you get a hot meal at lunchtime? Are you never taken into the house?"

I visited the office as requested and was offered a job with the Shorthorn herd at the Home Farm, lodging with the Aberdonian herdsman and his wife and children. Though the hours were long, the work was preferable to shawing neaps any day, and I was with Jim and his carter, Bob, for three years.'

There were, of course, animals on the general farms as Kathleen Ellis found:

'I was taken to a farm to do horse hoeing. The horse was a beautiful shire horse, he was lovely, more so than the farmer; why did I seem to get all the old miserable ones? However, at dinnertime, I got my packed lunch and looked for a warm place to sit, when the farmer asked me if I would like some fresh eggs. "Oh yes," said I and followed him to the hen hut. I was out in two seconds flat, telling him where to put his eggs. I had learned my first lesson. It was a very quiet afternoon and a very long one too, I think even the horse felt the tension.

One day at a farm I had to clean out the bull pen, Billy was his name. The farmer gave me a long stick with a hook on the end to get Billy by the ring on his nose and move him about whilst I cleaned his pen. I wasn't feeling exactly happy, but I managed. In my haste to get him safely back I didn't close the latch properly, and as Billy was cheesed off by then, he banged his head on the door and came after me. I ran like the wind, I saw a gate leading into a field, quickly opened it and stood back. Billy ran in and did he enjoy himself—I had let him into a field of heifers. I was never to go to that farm again!'

Mary Malloy too worked with animals:

'One farmer's wife bred turkeys for the Christmas trade, and a few weeks before these were due to be plucked, one or two disappeared every night or so. The farmer used to prowl around with a rifle but without success. However, the village policeman offered to keep his eye on things. During the night the farmer heard noises, dashed downstairs and seeing someone against the branches of an apple tree took a shot at the figure and to his horror discovered it was the arm of the law himself!...

I was given an old horse called "Bonny" to work with, but she took advantage of the fact that I was a "rookie" and much preferred standing still to walking. The farm was on the flight path of bombers returning from raids on Germany and each time one came in to land Bonny found it necessary to watch for several minutes, hence every job took twice as long as expected. The farmer eventually bought a tractor and I was taught to drive. Unfortunately my first attempt at driving proved a disaster, because upon coming to the hedge I shouted "Whoa" and the tractor went into the ditch.

One farmer and his wife used to go to market in a nearby town once a week and I was left on my own. On one occasion I was instructed to go to the field of turnips, take "a breed" and hoe the rows. About an hour later I was still in the implement shed looking for a breed and would still be there had the postman not called and informed me that a breed was the width of so many rows.

Another memory is of being kicked by a very spiteful horse. He caught me on the thigh and I crashed through a wooden partition right under the nose of the bull. He was so amazed that he just stood and looked at me, giving me time to make a hasty exit.'

Norah Welburn found that geese, too, were a hazard:

'I was sent to work for an elderly couple. After dinner I asked where the lavatory was. "Down at the bottom of the yard," the old man said, "but take the brush with you. Mrs Goose is sitting on her eggs and Mr Gander is very protective." So I set off with the brush in my hand. I'd got about halfway there when I saw him, head down, neck outstretched. I put the brush between him and me, but he just got hold of the bristles and pulled the brush straight out of my hand. I just managed to get into the loo. I was there for half an hour before the farmer came to release me. Every time I opened the door there was the goose, waiting.'

Dorothy Simpson too has cause to remember geese:

'I had barely unpacked, or so it seemed, when the lady of the house gave me one of my first jobs. She pointed to a flock of geese. "I want you to move them out of that meadow," she said, "round the front of the house, and into the field on the far side." I looked at the geese and the geese looked at me with cold sardonic eyes that scared me half to death.

Meanwhile, the farmer, too deaf to hear the knocking of my knees, was explaining, "Just throw your arms wide like this. Swing to the left and they'll go that way. Swing to the right and they'll go the other way." Well, this seemed simplicity itself and sure enough the geese moved out of the meadow like soldiers on parade. In the role of drill sergeant I did the arm bit and they rounded the house neatly. I was just congratulating myself upon this manoeuvre when disaster struck. The leader of the pack, an independent spirit, decided to head for the lane, and the rest followed him. "Stop, stop," I squealed, and he took no notice at all. The troop had become a disorderly rabble, spread out across the narrow lane and heading full tilt towards the village. I sprinted into the lead, waving my arms wildly, in a bid to effect an about turn. They ignored me completely. Another halfmile and the village was no longer distant.

In my fevered imagination I pictured geese invading the shops, the gardens, maybe even the houses... and some rustic Mr Plod enquiring, "Who be in charge of these 'ere birds?" We rounded the bend and the village was spread out before us.

At this point I spotted an open gate on our left and was just about to repeat my arm waving bit when the leader of the pack moved sedately through the gate without so much as a glance in my direction. The other geese, calmness restored, formed ranks and followed him back to the field. I walked behind them. I kept my arms down by my sides, hands in pockets, and spoke not a word. It seemed the wisest thing to do.'

Brenda Penfold had requested 'general farming' and two clear memories stay with her:

'I was on private farms, muck spreading in the fog with prisoners of war, and the sudden yell of, "Hey, that was me!" from the other workers... learning *Still is the Night* in German at 5.30 a.m. whilst bottling milk....'

Vera Campbell was willing to 'have a go' at anything:

Another job (under the supervision of an old man of 80) was to scythe thistles before they seeded; in a field with a bull in it. I used to think they wanted rid of the land girls, but this was one who stuck it out. The old man chewed black stuff in a roll—he cut off a piece and kept spitting it out. I was fascinated—of course I had to have a go, but being too much of a lady I did *not* spit and the result was I blackened out, sick as a dog—I bet I never lived it down....

Planting "tatties" (potatoes), and the picking months later, is a back-breaking job especially if pouring with rain and mud sticking to them. Harvest... was mostly done by hand, very little machinery.'

Oh how very innocent we were! Theo Rice, like the rest of us, found a lot to learn:

'I duly arrived a very "green" naive 19-year old townie. I blush to think of myself in those days. To illustrate, the first day we were walking around the duck pond with the farmer on our way to a midmorning break when I saw a duck on top of another, making quite a din. Horror-filled, I was on my way to part them crying out that one was getting hurt, when the incredulous expression on the farmer's face stopped me and realisation flooded in. Bette (my cousin) was laughing her socks off. Was my face red!...

I was told to feed Doris the mare her oats then shut her in for the night—I was to show Doris the oats at the appropriate time and she would follow me into her stall. It worked for five steps then Doris stalled. I stood on tiptoe and pulled her mane. I went behind and tried to push all to no avail and we were only a few yards from the stable. Then dear Doris turned and galloped right across the field to the farthest point where she waited until I caught up with her, puffing and blowing not knowing what to do next—next was Doris throwing her head back and whinnying—a real horse laugh—and galloping straight back into her stall leaving me to trudge back....

I transferred to arable farming at Tappington Hall, featured in the Ingoldsby Legends. Quite fun but whenever I had a date I had to immerse myself in the bath with my fresh clothes piled in the centre of the soap holder which spanned the bath, then up, dry, dress and out of the farmhouse in a flash in an endeavour to avoid carrying fleas. I never quite succeeded....

Early morning I had the job of feeding the animals. One morning half-awake and in the half dark I went into the barn and was about to plunge the hay fork into the hay but "something" stopped me. I stood wondering, then a slight movement in the hay—when my eyes were acclimatised I saw underneath the hay were some twenty soldiers. My blood ran cold as, had I plunged that deadly fork into the hay I would have seriously wounded, even killed. I was physically sick and I shiver now at the thought.'

Mary Phipps remembers Dirty Dick, a shire horse:

'I was helping out with the harvest, leading the horse and cart to the men building the hay rick. Nobody thought to tell me that he was splay footed and as I turned into the yard his front nearside hoof landed on my right toes. I was in agony, the men helped me onto his back, told me to go back to the house and get my foot seen to.... As I was going down the side of a very long field I suddenly lost my temper and kicked the horse in his side. Of course he bolted and we shot away.... We flew through the gates at the end and he stopped. I heard shouting and found the men racing towards me. They walked away muttering something about "bloody Londoners"... evidently the cart had only three inches clearance from the gateposts as we thundered through....

We were near the American airfields. They used to put things on the table in the cowshed while we were working, tins of peaches, cigarettes and lovely big bars of scented soap. I used to save most of it for my mum.... I was then taken to Terrington Marshes. It was Sunday and they were all sitting there while the dinner was served. I was really hungry. The foreman said, "Sit down girl." Well, I felt a bit ashamed at how much I was eating, but the foreman said, "You'll do, gal."'

Mary Horrobin was the rick builder during hay-making. Many a moonlit night they would be working to get the harvest in.

Joan Shakesheff was one of those who worked from a hostel, working at different farms as needed. The girls cycled everywhere, taking packed lunches and having tea or cider provided by the farmer—some farms of course didn't, and the girls sat outside in the damp cold, sometimes whilst Italian prisoners were invited into the house to have dinner. She goes on:

'You were often sent to farm alone, on general work, and found yourself facing a bull for the first time. The largest bull I ever saw was lying down in the byre, and being told to water the bull, I collected the largest bucket I have ever seen, having filled it from the pump outside, staggered across the yard, to hold it while the bull drank noisily. He plunged in his great head, trapping both my thumbs in doing so. I was relieved when he finally took a breath and released me....

On another farm I would take the bull for his exercise. He was quite docile and would amble up behind me but I objected to his friend, a smelly old goat who always followed. He had long shaggy hair down to the ground, if you were up wind it was terrible....

Over the years we did many different jobs, muck spreading, hoeing mangels and sugar beet in spring seemed to go on for ever.... I planted potatoes by hand at one farm... potato picking had us scrambling about, collecting them in buckets, transferring them into sacks at the end of the rows, hardly giving us a chance to clear them before the tractor came racing down again.... I disliked sprout picking, it was a wet cold job, they were often frozen and difficult to break off.... Fruit picking was a pleasant change in autumn, then there were odd jobs like stone picking— we picked enough stones from one field to make the pyramids.... Wet days saw us whitewashing cowsheds with huge brushes, coming away speckled with the stuff, or sitting on barn floors repairing corn sacks with huge bagging needles through which we threaded string. Sugar beet harvesting was a hard job, done during winter usually frozen in the ground, we had to get them out... we would boot them out with our heels, my heel is still painful sometimes after all these years.'

Ailsa Tanner echoes the sentiments expressed by so many about the patterns of stooks at harvest time:

'Hay was cut with a reaper which cut the grass in swathes. We then raked and turned it by hand with hay rakes made of wood, built it into little mounds called coils with a hay fork, most carefully, to let the rain run off, spread it out again to dry and when it was really dry, built it into large ricks in the field. When needed the rick was pulled onto a flat platform on wheels and taken with a horse to the hayloft in the farm.

Harvesting the corn was much the same but the reaper bound the sheaves with twine when they were big enough. Our job was to build stooks with six or eight sheaves placed firmly in pairs into the ground so that the stooks would not fall down. When they were dry enough they were loaded onto carts and large stacks were built in the stack yard, then thatched with "rashies" and roped down.

The best time at harvesting was the tea break, when the farm children came down from the farm with a large basket of girdle scones and butter and a big can of cold water with oatmeal floating in it—most refreshing.

There was a lot of hard work involved but the countryside looked so much more attractive at that time with the patterns of stooks and ricks over the fields. Now, great blocks of straw and polythene covered cylinders of hay, do not look the same at all, and what is most sad is that so few people are involved in farm work. Today all the hay forks, rakes, milking stools, luggies and even the carts and the horses that pulled them are lost or are now in museums, and I sometimes feel that I should be there with them!'

How the state of the weather and the time of year ruled our lives! Marjorie Harvey says:

'There are few better things than walking through the dewy grass in a cherry orchard midst the sheep and lambs in the early morning sun. However, there can also be few worse jobs when the weather is freezing. We had to chop tops off wurzles (for the horses) or cut brussel sprouts off their stalks etc. Frequently our hands stuck to the knives with the cold and tears poured down our cheeks with the pain. Another particular "fun" job was trying to light a bonfire with a heap of wet sticks and a few matches. Occasionally one or other of the farm labourers would take pity on us and light it with *one* match.'

Rene Hillier was one of those posted to a hostel named Larkstone, a lovely house which seems to have stayed in the memory of so many. Notice the sprouts again!

'The girls were a super bunch, of course some left and others took their places but on the whole we all got on very well together. As for the work, well it was jolly hard in those days, so much is done by machines now isn't it? The list is endless, we would go off in the lorry to different farms to do whatever job was in season, potato planting and picking, hedge clearing and burning, hay-making, harvesting and that awful job of threshing, muck spreading, hoeing sugar beet and mangel pulling. Even had a job picking up the stones from a big field.... Oh how I hated picking Brussels sprouts thick with frost!'

Marion Hinckley was on a mixed farm, that is, a bit of everything, in primitive conditions:

'... no electricity so it was oil lamps in the winter and no running water—it had to be hand pumped from the pond.'

Brenda Golden was a strong girl and found that this helped when it came to pitching sheaves all day:

'A winter job was riddling and bagging the potatoes. We occasionally sold off a bag or two to soldiers passing in a lorry who stopped and asked for them. We usually pocketed about 6*d.* each which we spent in the pub! The farmer didn't believe in pampering his staff. If a job could be done in rain, snow or bitter cold, we did it, along with our fellow farm workers. How grateful we were for our warm, waterproof WLA uniform items. For gloves I had a pair of fur-lined leather mittens inside which I could wear a pair of woollen gloves if necessary. Fencing with barbed wire was another job I helped with, and I could swing a sledge hammer with the best of them.'

'Our' farming world has gone, as Sheila Gordon-Rae says:

'I was put on the hay rake and told to rake the hayfield, which I somehow managed to do "sides to middle", which I'm sure gave the "useless land girls" judgement a boost.... Seeing all the machines at work these days makes me think of the hours I spent helping to build the hay and corn ricks, and how skilful the men were and how well they thatched them against winter.'

Phyllis Munn, a thatcher in season, turned her hand to other jobs at the onset of winter:

'Muck spreading, as the name might suggest, was not a task we approached with enthusiasm. The process consisted of heaving the repulsive stuff from a cart using a long-handled, fourpronged fork, and scattering it across the field. Another pursuit which has little to recommend it was pulling mangel wurzels. Stretching before us would be a large field of the beet in seemingly endless rows. In February, when the earth was hardened by frost, they would stubbornly resist our efforts to pull them out by hand, and a sharp kick from the toe of a gumboot would be the only way to dislodge them. On damp, dismal days, or when a vicious wind swept across the field and stung our faces until they ached, we were relieved when the winter light began to fade: then we could abandon the desolate scene with the huge piles of beet we had collected, and trudge thankfully across the sodden fields back to our host caravan and a hot meal.'

Norah Hawkes, however, has a sweet memory:

'Six of us went to a hostel in Long Campton where we were taken in an open trailer (very cold) to outlying farms.... A very old farmer dug up roots of snowdrops and gave them to us to take home to our mothers on Mothering Sunday.'

There were also differences in pay from county to county. Rose Motherdale says:

'Our days were busy but happy. I earned £2.7s.6d. a week and of this I paid £1 for my board.'

Whilst Marjorie Rossi says:

'I moved to Fulbourne in Cambridgeshire, working for three maiden ladies, Miss Sarah, Miss Sissy and Miss Edith. They were lovely to work for. We were paid 24/- a week, 18/- was taken for board.'

For Vivienne Passmore life was never dull:

'... in fact it was often hilarious.... I can visualise coming across our pleasant conscientious objector sitting on the carcase of a dead carthorse whilst concentrating on looking up its symptoms in some huge verterinary tome, in order to ascertain the cause of its demise.... Again, sorting swill from US army camps to be boiled for our pigs and finding a set of false teeth—no reward I'm afraid.'

It's the first time of doing anything that stays in the mind, as Joan Williams can testify:

'Our first job was to hoe a field of carrots. Naturally we chopped some of the tops off not being experienced at hoeing and we pushed them back in the ground, hoping the farmer would not notice but next morning all was revealed—withered carrot tops all over the field. Another job I had was rook-scaring. I had to run up and down a field of peas shouting and banging a tin to keep the birds off the peas. It was very hot that summer and those boots we were issued with seemed to weigh a ton.'

Marjorie Nesfield too, remembers her first day very clearly:

'... I was leading a horse and cart muck spreading. Needless to say having never led a horse, when turning at the end of the field the horse stood on my foot.... Despite cold winter days, frosty mornings pulling sugar beet, dusty threshing days, hot days in a Dutch barn topping them up when hay and straw had settled, I would do it all again.'

Fortunately Joan Law's sense of humour seems to have been equal to the task:

'Every morning I used to cycle to work at the crack of dawn. The bikes we were issued with were the heaviest I have ever seen. It was always dark and every morning I used to go over a pot hole and my lamp went out and every morning the same policeman (never saw him), just his voice, saying, "Your light's out, Miss." I could have put his lights out very often.

One day we had to go through a paddock with the bull in it, we climbed on the horse to get through. Halfway across Andy started slipping down the back of the horse taking me with her. We landed in a heap at the bull's feet. He looked at us with contempt and turned away. So much for us!'

Threshing too seems to belong to another world. It was a filthy, noisy job. Yvonne Timbs:

'... a huge dirty machine, had to throw sheaves of wheat up, then it was threshed into corn. Dust, mice, lugging bags of corn, it nearly killed us city girls—so soft we couldn't even lift our arms to comb our hair without groaning. We rang the powers-that-be and said we couldn't take it and wanted to go home! Naturally in no uncertain terms we got a stern lecture and eventually we became used to it.'

Others travelled with the machine, as did I. G. Thompson:

'... threshing was hard, but I teamed up with another girl and we went to many different farms with the same farm workers travelling with the "drum"—the farmer was hired by the War Agricultural Department and I suppose you'd call it contracted out. His threshing machine was the only one in the area. We were paid a shilling a day extra for threshing!'

Phyllis Weston remembers a dramatic harvest:

'One day we were on a farm working overtime to do harvesting and someone dropped a lighted match and caught all the field of corn alight, so before they could get the fire engines to come we all had to beat out the flames and we were black with soot. That was our overtime for that night. A few days later the farmer sent us all one shilling and sixpence for our help that night.'

Everyone was pressed into service at harvest time, as Connie McNichol recalls:

'One of my favourite places was Kinharvie, an estate owned by the Dowager Duchess of Norfolk at that time, where there was electricity in the byre for the cows, but not in the grieve's house at the home farm. I had the distinction one time of making stooks with the then Duke of Norfolk, who wore a lovely blue linen shirt which I coveted no end. Never having met a duke before, I thought that, for once in my life, I had better not speak till spoken to! Unfortunately the Duke was either very shy or very surly and he addressed not a single word to me. After about half an hour of stony silence His Grace suddenly shot off the field and was not seen again, much to the amusement of the other farm workers.'

Betty Cutts also went threshing:

'Threshing was a terrible job in those days as one woke up in the mornings feeling as if you had swallowed a hedgehog, from the dust and chaff.'

Lilian Gerber, now in Niagara Falls, writes that her first job was in a four-acre field of sugar beet, 'What a surprise!' and:

'...from there I was transferred to East Grinstead and spent the rest of my time on a threshing machine which was driven by an old circus tractor.... Everyone said hoeing was very monotonous, it certainly didn't look like it, and looked easy, but how I remember using a hand hoe for baby carrots—what a horrible job.'

Enid Bennell gives a wry look at farming past and present, including the ubiquitous threshing:

'Some had training as promised, some didn't—I didn't. They just drove us all in a canvas-topped lorry to various farms, there we were given a hoe and told to chop out the weeds between the sugar beet. I admired the townies, it couldn't have been that easy for them to plunge themselves from town life to the somewhat boggy countryside and all that goes with it. As for me, I'm a country girl so I knew, a pea from a puddle as you might say.

Some farmers thought they were on to a good thing with us rookies, they certainly tried the strong arm tactics. I guess we retaliated, being youngsters, but most farmers I think were very good to us. These days if you look at any area of farming it's a different kettle of fish to what we knew. Today even a bloke pushing a lawn mower wears noise protection on his ears. Everything is so mechanized these days, all you want is a brain to go with it, no brawn is needed any more.

That's where our farming comes in doesn't it? Take milking, done by hand, put through a cooler, then into churns and those churns so heavy you had to roll them, then put them in a cart and take them to the stand to await the lorry for collection.

Now muck spreading—all dung was forked into a cart from a muck heap in the farm yard and taken to the fields by horse where we forked it over the fields. Today it's a muck spreader which does it in half the time. Nearly everything needed hand lifting those days, no mechanical lifts. Some girls worked in gangs as I did, until I drove tractors. Jobs consisted of hoeing, where we worked in rows up and down the fields. It did get boring but a trip behind the haystack and a cigarette eased the situation. These gangs travelled from farm to farm until jobs of the season were completed, so in a year we covered quite a few farms and made a lot of friends with farmers and workers.

Potato planting and picking was a real slog, sack aprons which at times nearly broke our backs and the mud on our Land Army boots—gosh, did our feet ache! Now potato sorting, imagine riddling potatoes in a wide open field in the cold and wet of the winters, all potatoes were clamped along the edge of the fields. Today they are brought in and bagged up.

Another winter job which froze most of us to the bones was hedging and ditching. We slashed those hedges to keep warm, burning the trimmings was lovely to stand round. I remember toasting our spam sandwiches over the flames by means of a stick, black and burnt they may have been but they tasted good. Now hedges are machined and hacked.

Then there's harvesting, long and drawn out from farm to farm again. Horse and wagon, pitch forks, old fashioned reapers, not a combine in sight. We stooked the corn to dry, walking round and round the fields then carting and pitching onto the wagons and hoping it wouldn't fall off. We took it back to the farm yard or nearest field to stack so it was pitched onto an elevator and taken to the stack to be laid out, then later on it was thatched.

Now threshing, what a hard mucky job! A smoke-belching steam engine moving belts that burnt you if you happened to touch them, dust off the chaff and cavings as we tried to rake it clear from the thresher. We really got filthy, it got into our eyes, down our throats, up our noses and in our clothes, not forgetting our hair. We looked like total wrecks by the end of the day and a bath at the end of it was heaven.

We took it in turns threshing, so the next thing was cutting the bonds up top and feeding the drum. The corn comes up and spits in your face which certainly stings. And lastly baling, that entails feeding wires through the machine, as the straw came out it was compressed into bales and the wires held them together. We girls carried these heavy bales to make a stack. When it got high we climbed a ladder with them—that was not funny especially when you did it day in and day out. Farmers don't harvest like that now, it's combines, using wagon and tractor for the corn, no bales of straw. I tell you if we weren't tough to start with we were when we had finished.'

W. M. Debenham writes that she chose the Land Army rather than factory work and in spite of everything liked the outdoor life:

'My first experience was walking through fields of thick snow in Wellington boots to help clear land for crops, then it was just as hard in muddy fields when the snow melted, but it gave us good appetites.'

Joan Baker was sent to a large farm in Diss, Norfolk—no, not sugar beet:

'... specialising in grain production and the fattening of beef cattle but no dairy cattle. There were three other land girls employed, they were billeted out with the families of the farmhands, I was put up with the farmer and family in the main farmhouse. Our farm was the first in the area to have its own combine harvester for our own use and for hiring out to neighbouring farms. I was taught to drive the tractors ready for harvest time.

My main job was to look after the large herd of bullocks. The railway line ran alongside the main grazing and I still have vivid memories of battling grass fires at all hours days and nights after sparks from the railway engines had set the field afire. Other memories are of riding the farmer's hunter down to the village blacksmith to be shod, doing quite a deal of baby-sitting for the farmer and his wife, but the worst memory is of helping to take the fattened bullocks to market on their way to slaughter.'

The farmers, too, seem to have left a great impression. Evelyn Waight, for instance, names the farmer as the drawback:

'... an obnoxious man, who had been put into farming by his father—a baker—in order to dispose of some of his excess money and keep an eye on his son. He had no idea of farm work, constantly made a fool of himself, used the royal "we" when planning overtime, but never actually turned up, and worked a fiddle on clothing coupons and our harvest rations.'

Daphne Jauncey and her friends, however, managed to hold their own:

'Our man in charge was a Mr Tickner, nicknamed Hitler—well he did have a moustache, even if it was ginger! What a life we led him, we all used to spend more pennies than necessary, we enjoyed the long walks to find a hedge.'

Sometimes a farmer turned up trumps, as D. L. King says:

'At one farm the foreman asked me to take the tractor in the brew to feed the bullocks. It had been a wet morning and my Wellingtons were wet at the bottom. On driving into the building the bullocks all crowded round to get to the feed. On driving forward my foot slipped on the clutch and I shot forward knocking down one of the animals.... The foreman was in a terrible state, all sorts of things were going to happen to me, including having to pay for the beast... anyway the farmer said that the space in the brew was too small to turn the tractor and I shouldn't have been sent there in the first place.'

Betty Ambler found that the role of farmer's wife made a great deal of difference to the girls' working day:

'The farmers were very good to us and when we were in the fields during the morning the farmer's wife would come along with a basket of sandwiches, hard-boiled eggs, scones and cakes and a big can of tea, and this used to happen if we were still there in the afternoon. It was very much appreciated as we had very big appetites when we were young and working in the fresh air all day.'

Irene Abbott too comments on the kindness of those she worked with—and she includes the cart horses in that:

'... the kindness and patience of most of those we worked with, for we were, with a few exceptions, very green. Also the skill of those gentle giants the cart horses, an animal I have a very soft spot for. They knew better than us how to get their load through a gateway without taking down the gatepost, be it a four-wheeled wagon, or two-wheeled cart they pulled, and they would stop dead if we were not swinging wide enough.'

Betty Arbon too remembers the good nature shown towards the 'green' girls:

'There were about 40 people working in the fields. Ian, a trainee farmer, was with us and he was extremely kind and got us through our first day, which they called "swede bashing". We felt utterly stupid.... It got to 9 a.m. and we were told it was lousing time. By this time the locals were very kind and invited us to "louse" with them, which turned out to be morning lunch time. We shared our pack which was always the same—a huge chunk of bread pudding and a bottle of cold tea. We were very hungry. We had an hour break then we were told to follow if we wanted to relieve ourselves. Toilets, we thought, good news. But no such luck, just a field with a high hedge... then it began to rain, it bucketed down. Our hair hung round our faces and our clothes clung to us.... We really did not know what we were doing. All I knew about harvest was harvest festivals. To the farmer it was "panic time". To me it was heat, thistles, torn hands, flies and killing rabbits.'

We all have memories of episodes which at the time seemed anything but funny but are now recalled with smiles, as Doreen Butler says:

'My friend taking the overhead bin out to the midden after mucking out the byre, in the blackout she fell in the midden and came back dripping in muck. I had to hose her down with cold water at 5 o'clock on a February morning. It was not funny for Ellie but gave the rest of us a good laugh. I can still see it dripping off her glasses... the girl who fed a pig for a week when it was dead. When asked how she did not see this her reply was, "I don't like pigs and just tossed the food in without looking".'

Win Smith must have been frightened by her adventure at silage time, but now it is a good story for the grandchildren:

'I had been sent to a small farm to help make silage. There was only one man working the farm, which was owned by two elderly ladies. The silo was installed in an old barn. We backed the horse and cart into the barn and the chappie climbed a ladder and got into the silo. I took the ladder and placed it by the side of the loaded cart and climbed up on to the top of the load prepared to start unloading into the silo. The chappie called out to wait a moment whilst he trod the silage down. I was as high as the rafters so put my pitchfork into the load and sat on the rafters. I don't know what caused it but the horse ambled off taking the load with it and leaving me hanging on the rafters. Without thinking I jumped—it must have been all of 15 feet. Why I didn't break a leg I don't know but thinking about it afterwards if I had stopped to think I would never have had the courage to jump, and there was no one about to help—the only one who could have done was in the silo—he was more shaken than I was!'

Weather, of course, ruled our work. We may have hoped, with Dorothy Simpson, that bad weather meant no work. We had a lot to learn:

'There was an instance one winter when overnight the snow had fallen. Our hostel was a ten minute walk up a rough drive to the lane. One of the girls ventured out and found the snow had come over the top of her gum boots, so with great glee we all settled in for a comfortable day at home. Not so! The farmer sent a tractor with trailer behind, and we all had to get in the trailer and were taken by tractor to the orchard, where in the freezing cold and knee-high in snow, we had the job of scraping the loose bark from the trees where the insects were hiding. Never have I been so cold, standing all day with hardly any movement and nothing to get the circulation going.'

Sometimes it was the enmity of inanimate objects that made us fume as Elsie Druce found:

'We went off on our bikes which were plain and sturdy, a bit heavy and no three speeds. Windy days we hated pushing along against the wind, sometimes tempers got the better of us and we would hurl them into the ditch, but it didn't do any good because we had to climb in and get them out again.

Our first job was loading up a trailer with fresh (very fresh) manure. None of us had ever had anything to do with this commodity before and most of that first morning we took it in turn to be sick. But as the days got sunny and the stuff got drier and drier we got to like the job, and even got so far as to sit on it to eat our lunch.'

Sometimes, of course, the objects were anything but inanimate and Joan Clifford says:

'I used to work with three horses, Prince, Bluebird and The Colt. My first job was to fetch these huge farm horses from the field each morning. All went well until one morning I had the halters on Prince and The Colt, but Bluebird wouldn't come, and as I stood there holding a horse each side of me, ears back, it suddenly charged straight at me. He could only have been about 12 yards from me—I threw up my arms and shouted the first thing that came into my head—"Scram". The enormous animal was so surprised that he skidded to a halt and as I walked the other two down into the village the rebel followed. When I told the farmer what had happened, he said, "Oh, has he started that with you—a pity." I asked him why he hadn't told me what he was like and he said, "If I had told you before, you wouldn't have fetched him would you?"

One afternoon I found the bull had got out of his pen at the end of the cowshed. He was a nasty animal and had a long chain fastened to the ring in his nose. I managed to shut the doors to prevent him getting out into the village, and got behind the stalls where the cows were to be milked and managed to lean over and grab the chain. I pulled him back into his own pen into which I had climbed, then got out and shut the gate. It wasn't until a few minutes later that I realised what a stupid thing I had done pulled the bull in by his chain with my back to the wall of his pen! It was some time before I stopped shaking.

I used to carry 2½ cwt bags of meal and corn on my back and have suffered with severe back problems ever since.'

And how about Pat Warren's stories of jobs which might not be thought suitable for a woman:

'We had a bush clearing job in the winter and had enormous fires after which I was given a blueprint of a drainage system to be carried out. The girls had to dig clay out and throw it on top of the bank. By the time we had gone down nearly 5 ft it took two people to pull the girls out at the end of the day. To earn our money we were expected to complete half a chain each.

Potton Island consisted of a small arable farm where my gang was sent. We had to row over if the tide was in, otherwise use a small causeway. We worked some 16 hours a day during harvest time and drove home in a lorry at 9 o'clock, had dinner and fell into bed.... Charlie the horse decided he didn't like the planks we were loading as he could see them over his blinkers—as he moved the cart and the planks clapped together and this was too much for him.

He took off with me holding the reins in both hands, feet braced against the cart front. We rounded the rough bricked approach to the farmyard and went past the duck pond, occasionally on one wheel. The noise was horrendous, in spite of this, those workers who weren't leaping for their lives were giving me plenty of advice, none of which I could hear except one who yelled "Jump". I preferred to stay where I was, didn't fancy the duck pond or the rough broken bricks. We finished up in the barn both shaking until the men appeared.

I noticed a little respect had appeared at last and I felt one of them rather than the girl! One of the bright sparks said, "You looked just like bloody Boadicea!"

General farming has its problems. I managed to have a foot almost crushed when I dangled my feet over the front of a trailer as the tractor changed course, and later, when I had the horse and cart, a load I was moving came off as I was on top and the whole thing slid off. A gentle landing on straw saved broken bones but the pitchfork went through my wellie boot, my two pairs of socks and right calf, but missed all vital veins, arteries and bones and it was a clean fork.'

Doreen Leibrandt still has her old kitbag now filled with memories:

'... blisters on hands and feet, the sunburn even on your legs. The wasp and bee and nettle stings along with all the other strange plants and insects that came as quite a shock for a city girl.

My next posting meant a move to Brighton and from here we generally worked at Saltdean. One evening returning on the bus we were very firmly sent upstairs as the little old ladies aboard did not appreciate the aroma of muck spreading land girls!'

Joan Welbourn's job was an unusual one:

'Our job was to look after the potato clamps at the site near Llanfair station. The farmers brought their wagons to be weighed which we had to check. Potatoes put in different clamps whichever variety, King Edwards, Red King, Majestic, Doone Star, Great Scot etc. Then the Committee paid the grower on behalf of the Ministry of Food.'

Dorothy Chard, after being trained and sent to a dairy farm, transferred to be nearer home:

'Harvest time was a real challenge, one worked all the daylight hours—15 and 16 hours were the normal. Everything pulled or driven by two wonderful horses, Sam and Boxer.... When the corn was cut we would go in to make it into stooks and hand bind them.... Helping to make the stack was all right until you came to the very top. With the sun beating down relentlessly on the corrugated roof it was red hot and if you caught your arms and back you certainly knew it! I helped plant and pick potatoes and welcomed the trains that passed to wave to the holidaymakers with that excuse to ease the pain in my back.'

Vera Calf was billeted near Walsingham with girls from Bradford and Leeds—what a change this must have been!

'We weeded the fields, worked on sugar beet, feeding the bullocks, chopping logs, washing the farmer's kitchen floor and cleaning the farmhouse windows.'

This domestic work for the farmer was not, of course, what we were supposed to do. E. V. Campion too put in some time on these chores:

'It was on Dartmoor and very isolated. After working all day on the farm I had to draw water from a pump in the yard, fill up several cast-iron cauldrons, hang them over an open fire, and when the water was hot, bath their children. It got too much. I think that memory lingers because it was probably the only unpleasant one.'

Norah Hawkes worked on a mixed farm:

'... growing corn, sugar beet, etc., rearing bullocks, sheep, a few pigs and poultry. Just the farmer, an old man and myself with help at threshing etc. by gangs of Italian and German prisoners and land girls.... It was an interesting time, but hard. The endless hours carrying straw, hay to cattle and sheep through snow and bad weather, particularly in 1947 when the village was cut off for weeks with snowdrifts. But there was great satisfaction after helping at lambing, gathering in the harvest etc. and now at over 70 I wish I was young enough to return to it!'

In a contribution to a local newspaper Norah Golden says:

'We were in a field picking potatoes when someone said, "Hey, there's a combine!" We all rushed to the edge to look at this strange monster come by. I had an awful premonition then that farming as I knew it had come to an end.... Women did every job imaginable, whatever a man would have done, there were no concessions.'

In case anyone still thinks it was all wine and roses Betty Schibler reminds us of the nearness of disaster:

'There were bikes provided to take us to work on some nearer farms and one morning the two who came from London, Olive and Joan, who were great friends, set off on two bikes. While going down hill Olive's brakes failed and she crashed into a six foot brick wall which instantly killed her. Joan was devastated but carried on with her work. Shortly afterwards while Joan was driving a farm tractor it overturned and killed her instantly. Who will be next, we all wondered?'

Agnes Aspinall too has a sad memory:

'While I was on a farm called Shellacres we were working in a harvest field. It had just been all cut when one of the young men was killed by his own tractor. I can't remember how it happened. He lived with his mother and brother in the cottage next to ours, you can imagine how shocked and upset we all were.'

13

TRACTOR DRIVING

Not all of us had an opportunity to drive a tractor—I muffed my chance. Whilst training we were taken to a sloping field for muck spreading and there was a small caterpillar tractor to which was hooked a trailer piled high with—you've guessed it—manure. 'Hop on,' I was told, and duly hopped on to the tractor. 'You pulls this, and turns that,' but when I did so the trailer took a list to starboard and the manure tumbled slowly, oh so slowly, down the slope. Oh well, it was good while it lasted!

Doris Hall, working on a farm, was learning to drive the tractor for the first time:

'We went up and down the field three times—the chappie said, "Now, do you think you can manage it?" "Oh, yes," I said, "no problem." With that he jumped off saying, "I'm just off home for a cup of tea." I think I must have circuited the field 100 times before he reappeared. "But you didn't tell me how to stop it!"'

His reply is not recorded.

Marjorie Harvey was given the opportunity to drive the tractor, none of which in those days was equipped with a self-starter or a cabin:

'There's nothing quite equal to starting a tractor with a starting handle about 6.30 a.m. on a winter's morning (remembering to keep your thumb on the right side as they certainly had a kick) to warm you up.

Ellen Wood also found that taking on tractor driving was something entirely new:

'When we first went to the farms to do work for them they didn't really take to the fact that girls could do ploughing etc. so we had to prove it to them. But having once done so, they were really good to us and helped whenever they could.... One bad winter we went out with snow ploughs on our tractors and kept the roads in the vicinity clear.... We had Fordson tractors and had to keep them in good order. It was hard work but well worth it looking over the land you've just worked.'

Nancy Johnson:

'When I see modern day tractors I am filled with envy—built-in cabs, self-starters, radios and hydraulic lifts. I began driving a Fordson, heavy handles to swing for starting, especially difficult in winter. It was virtually impossible to keep warm, in severe weather I would wrap sacks around my shoulders and legs in a vain attempt to keep out the bitter cold winds. On one occasion I remember pulling off my boots and was warming my feet on the remains of a bonfire when my socks started burning—my feet were so cold I hadn't felt the heat!... I had to spend the whole evening mending my precious LA socks.

As a contrast in summer in prolonged hot weather I was almost blinded by the dirt and dust, at the end of the day eyes peered out from a blackened face. It would have been heaven to have gone home each evening to a bath, but although I was lucky and billeted in a comparatively modern house (it had a bathroom) the fuel for heating water was rationed, and bearing in mind there were seven of us in the household, we only managed one bath per person per week.

During the harvest I worked very long hours, it was double summer time and I would start at seven in the morning and often continue until eleven at night. I would have an hour off for lunch when a relief driver would take over. Probably a jam sandwich and a bottle of cold tea would be the mainstay for a ten minute break at 5 o'clock, the jam would have soaked into the bread making it fairly revolting, but I don't remember thinking so at the time—I was hungry! Sometimes if we were working near habitation householders would bring out a fresh cup of tea which was wonderful.

Over the years I drove several types of tractor, Fordson, Allis Chalmers, Ferguson, Ransome and in latter years a Caterpillar.... One incident I remember clearly, we had a field in the village, part of which was taken over by the War Office as a POW camp. Towards the end of the war the land was reclaimed and I was sent with Caterpillar and cultivator to level off the land. Unknown to me the prisoners had dug a cesspool and of course camouflaged the top. As I was driving across the front of the tractor suddenly lurched down into the large hole and being on tracks it left me in a very unnatural vertical position. I must have thought that the ground was going to swallow me up as I remember throwing the tractor out of gear, jumping off, and running for dear life to a nearby barn. When I ventured to look again the tractor was three parts submerged and the farmer had to hire lifting tackle to rescue it.'

Memories of starting up on cold mornings seem to have remained with most of the drivers. Dorothy Fox reported to the Agricultural Depot at Usk and:

'...some of us were sent to the Machinery Depot just outside Abergavenny, where girls who were experienced tractor drivers took us with them each day, to instruct us how to drive tractors and use other types of machinery. The tractors were the old type Fordsons, with just a choke, clutch and a starting handle with which to start the engine—not easy on cold frosty mornings. Our work consisted of going out with experienced tractor drivers to work on farms, threshing, ploughing. harrowing and baling. When we were threshing we worked with a chap who took a threshing drum to farms in the area until all the corn had been threshed.'

Over-eagerness, however, could cause difficulties as M. Smith found:

'I was sent to harvest a field of corn and did so in good time, so I decided to do the next field as well, and I also stooked the sheaves up lovely. To my horror I discovered the second field was not ours and the corn was not ready to be harvested for another week, so a large bill had to be paid to the other farmer.

On another occasion we had to firewatch one night a week and this night it started at 3 a.m., all clear at 6.15 a.m., so not much sleep as had to go off work just as usual. After lunch (a sandwich) I decided to carry on harrowing this field, in the middle of nowhere, fell off to sleep on my tractor, finished up in a hawthorn hedge and slept for an hour or more. When I came to fortunately the tractor was still running. In those days we had to crank the engine to start and both of us in the middle of the hawthorn hedge—it took me ages to get us both out!'

Brenda Penfold remembers the bad times:

'For instance I turned my tractor over into a dyke down on the Sandwich "Flats" as they were then known. The earth was very fine and I was harrowing and turned a corner too fast, the exhaust on top of the tractor saved me from serious injury, and I was able to clamber out from under to crawl to the top of the dyke where I could see the girls from other areas running to see if I was OK. It took a Caterpillar to pull the tractor back up and get it back to the yard, and I had to keep turning the engine by hand and removing the plugs and cleaning the oil off them for a few days before I got my tractor going again, a lesson well learnt I can tell you!'

Laura Oliver helped to lay tracks for the railway at the MOD site and Ruddington:

'...that was OK as we got extra pay. Then I went to work for the War Agricultural Committee spraying fruit trees. They asked me if I could drive a tractor and I said yes, though I had never been on one, so when I got to the first orchard there stood a Caterpillar tractor. I said, "I haven't driven that type before," so I watched every move he made. That seemed OK till we had finished spraying then he said, "Go and start the Fordson up ready to move on." You can imagine how I felt but luck was with me again—I was fiddling about with it for about half an hour. I said, "There must be something wrong with it." He tried and it wouldn't start so I was off the hook again.'

Ivy Walker says she instituted the first post office robbery:

'... by catching the PO van on my tractor tow bar and went sailing merrily through the village, with the postman doing a four minute mile in the rear.'

Audrey Sykes gives details of the updating of farmwork:

'It was traditional in Sussex to have the potatoes planted by Good Friday. This was done by hand initially, walking up and down the furrows, filling one's bucket from bags of seed potatoes placed at intervals, and dropping one potato in front of each foot as one moved down the field, refilling the bucket as one came to the next bag. The furrows were then filled in, usually by Janet and her Ferguson tractor. I believe we had the first one in Sussex at the Manor, and very nippy little machines they were. Later on we had a mechanical potato planter which did two rows at a time, with four of us sitting dropping the potatoes down the chutes and into the furrows being made as we proceeded down the field, being covered up as they landed in the soil, all in one operation.

The only problem as far as we were concerned were the dreadful fumes from the tractor. Nobody thought the pollution might he bad for us, so we just got on with it, but not without many grumbles! It was the same with the cabbage planter, another mechanical wonder, working on the same principle as the potato planter but this time we laid the plants between two rubber covered "fingers", which held them upright as two angled wheels pressed them firmly into the ground. In dry conditions the plants could be watered in from a tank on the top of the machine, with flaps that opened and shut as the plant was heeled in. Not as back-breaking as having to dib them in, as we did in my first year or so, gangs of us moving down the field and back.'

Joan Hawell started tractor driving for the War Agricultural Committee on a farm they had taken over for the duration of the war which had not been cultivated to the standards required in wartime:

'Until now my tractor driving experience had been with the old green Standard Fordson. They never felt inclined to start on a cold morning but always did if the cranking handle was turned for long enough. Most of the machinery was also quite old. As I was now driving for the Committee I had far superior equipment to any I had used before. The grey Ferguson was a joy to start with just a press of a button. I was probably one of the first WLA girls to drive a combine for harvesting.'

Even after training I. Pamphlett found it was hard to drive a tractor:

'... as you could only start it by swinging the handle, and they had a back kick, and also used to flood easily.... I was hired out to any farm that needed me to do their tractor work. I enjoyed that very much as I felt I was my own boss and got joy out of seeing a field nicely ploughed.'

Audrey Manning seems to have been given a very abridged training:

'After ten minutes tuition I was alone on the Fordson, harrowing and rolling as if I had been doing it for years. That night I remember dreaming I was driving round and round a field and woke up sitting on the side of the bed shouting, "I can't stop, I can't stop."

Tractors weren't only in use in farms, however, as Gladys Levingbird recounts:

'After a while they wanted a tractor driver's mate and I was assigned to Jack who had a tractor and trailer on the road. There was a tank-trap that had been made across parts of Essex (Epping, Chigwell, etc.) and it was our job to move the equipment and caravan and bulldozer, as the person driving the bulldozer knocked down these concrete blocks, and then had to be moved further along the road. The bulldozer had to be driven onto our trailer. I was then taught to drive a tractor where I had a provisional licence to take it on the road.'

Barbara Ould says she is:

'... still in touch with my original employers in Herefordshire—even though they remind me that I didn't quite succeed in getting a six foot wide tractor trailer through a seven foot gate!'

14

MARKET GARDENING

My first posting was to a hotel in Leatherhead to grow food for the guests, mostly old ladies who had removed from London. I slept at an ex-gardener's cottage but ate at the hotel—very good, and the bread and dripping for elevenses was mouth-watering, not that the old ladies would have thought so!

Percy, the gardener, hadn't been too keen on having a land girl but really had not much option so made a rather sullen best of it. The kitchen garden was screened from guests' eyes and rows of vegetables stood to attention for Percy, but wilted for me. Gravel paths everywhere had to be hand weeded and when another land girl (Mag) joined me we each sat on an upturned bucket pulling up stubborn weeds. Percy had no conversation and his orders were always in the same phrases; at the end of the day dismissal was, "Let's see what tomorrow brings forth", and when fallen leaves had to be swept it was always, "Take yer broom, and yer barrer, and yer boards—".

One thing we did hate was pushing the roller over the tennis courts and it was this I think which made me apply for a transfer still in market gardening, and I was posted to Shamley Green in Surrey. Six land girls already worked there, together with local girls and an under call-up aged lad. The main crop was tomatoes and oh the smell of them now takes me straight back to those endless hours of watering, taking the shoots out, and eventually picking them ending up with hands, arms, clothes and hair besmeared with green and smelling like a harvest festival.

Outside the greenhouses we hoed and hoed and hoed. Mary Becraft, too, found the colouring from the tomatoes very trying:

'My first assignment was at Chingford, Essex, to a tomato grower—a Mr Rumsey. There were about 30 greenhouses and hundreds of plants. We used to bath every night as the smell lingered on and we were covered in a kind of yellow dye from the plants. It really stained us, and everything we wore.'

Molly Hefford also worked in Surrey—it wasn't an easy option:

'Two of my friends at the Coal Commission joined with me in June 1941 and we were sent to Walton-on-Thames to a market garden. We lived in a hostel, Devoke Lodge.... There were two gangs in the garden... life was hard and in double summer time we got up at 4 a.m. to cut lettuce for the Covent Garden market. We then went back for breakfast and off out by 7 a.m. to pick tomatoes and push-hoe. A lot of our work was piece work, but generally we had about 30/- wages after we paid for our hostel.

Winter was hard, we brushed the snow off carrots before we could dig them up, and the leeks and sprouts were frozen in the ground. Kohl rabi was grown for cattle feed. The film crew came down and took a movie of all of us, and generally when you see the WLA on TV it has us all in it like a line of chorus girls, with dungarees, and scarves around our heads.'

Doris Hall was offered a job at a vicarage:

'The vicar was a hard task master. He gave me a certain amount of work to finish each day—sometimes I was still digging or planting until seven or eight in the evening. In the mornings I was called at 6 a.m. and at 6.30 he was waiting on the back step with a watch in his hand, and woe betide me if I was a few minutes late! It did me no harm and I stuck it for six months.'

At that time many hospitals had enough ground in which to grow fruit and vegetables to feed the patients—no prizes for guessing who helped with the growing, supplementing labour from men both over and under the age of call-up. Betty Arbon was one of those who worked in the grounds of a sanatorium:

'... where there were acres of gardens and ground. It was self supporting and helped out with other places. We had just a staff of head gardener, me and a boy.... We grew everything. We had a large greenhouse for tomatoes, cucumber and mushrooms, a field for hay, vegetables, soft fruit of every kind, a small orchard with apples, plums, pears etc. We kept chickens, turkeys, geese and rabbits. The flower beds were always the same as we took all our own seed—forget-me-nots, daisies, pansies and geraniums and of course roses and sweet peas.'

Marjorie James worked in a corporation park which, however, grew food crops in response to the call to 'Dig for Victory':

'I worked there, sometimes in the open fields, back-breaking work planting leeks, hoeing beet etc. sometimes in the greenhouses where hothouse fruit was grown, mostly for civic functions, Mayor's receptions etc.'

Vera Campbell worked on a town park in Aberdeen given over to producing foods:

> 'I was transferred into town and worked with a squad of women for weeding and hoeing; then our produce went to the British restaurants. I had the job of delivering of "tatties" (potatoes), lettuce, sprouts, cabbages, leeks, carrots etc. The "neaps" (turnips) were harvested later.'

Branwen Weekes, rather like a cook, learnt how to follow written directions, but the phrase she uses, "alternately loving it and hating it", strikes home:

> 'Three of us were sent to Tenby and each of us was assigned to a private garden where the gardener had been called up into the forces. We were outraged. Had we not answered the clarion call to serve King and country? This was not at all what we had expected. However, a whole new world was opened to us of nannies and housekeepers, parlour maids and butlers never before encountered except in books. A shilling an hour for a 44-hour week was what we were paid and 10/6d of this went to pay the rent for a flat the three of us shared in a large country house just outside Tenby. We augmented our rations with gardeners' perks so we never went short of fruit or vegetables, although we were rather disappointed to find that the mistress of the house had actually counted the peaches on the espalier tree in the walled garden, so we never had those luxuries on our menu.
>
> Our first week was not a full one and my friend Anne, who worked for a family of the butler keeping class, was faced at the end of the week by a very worried-looking lady. She had worked out what was owed and was unable to put a halfpenny on the cheque. "Think nothing of it," said Anne generously. She had no idea what she was going to do with this cheque anyway since not one of us had a bank account, but it amounted to a halfpenny less rather than a halfpenny more than she had earned.
>
> My bible was called *How to Grow and Produce your own Food*. A guide illustrated with lino cuts and rather nice pen and ink drawings. Propped up in the greenhouse it gave me instructions on handling spade and fork, digging, bastard trenching and deep trenching. It told me how to make a drill, how to sow and label seeds, how far apart to plant cabbages and cauliflowers and leeks and potatoes and other things I'd never even heard of, and all about animal and vegetable manures. It listed remedies against Enemies of Vegetable Crops and, yes, the tried and tested method of catching wireworm was there.
>
> I learnt to hoe the gravel drives, to mow the lawn, to plant out the flower beds, to prune the fruit trees and the roses and a thousand and one other things. But by the middle of the year Anne and I had become more confident and increasingly dissatisfied with our jobs as private gardeners in time of war. We told the powers-that-be that we hadn't given up our immensely important work in the Civil Service

to be treated in such a way and that we expected to be given more important things to do. So they gave us another large garden belonging to another large house, but this time it was to be part of the war effort and the fruit and vegetables that we grew were to be sold in the shops and in the market in Tenby and this time we worked together.

They were happy days that summer. The book was still propped up in the greenhouse. "Being a native of the seaside asparagus appreciates seaweed", it said. Great news. We spent days on the beach hacking it off the rocks and trundling it in barrow loads back to the garden. We sowed and planted and harvested and grew browner each day as we worked in the lovely soft breezes that came from the sea.

Then came winter. "Vines need their bark stripping", it said. More good news. We spent days in the comfort of the warm greenhouse doing just that. But all this pleasure was cancelled out when it came to picking sprouts and spinach on a frosty morning. The misery of it is hard to imagine and afterwards, lying on the staging in the greenhouse over the hot water pipes, nursing our bruised and aching fingers we vowed to join the ATS, the WAAF or the WRNS. But we stuck it out, alternately loving it and hating it until in 1944, when my mother died, I went back to Cardiff to have a stab at housekeeping for father.'

Molly Andrew worked in greenhouses among the ubiquitous tomatoes:

'We would also do fruit and pea picking, my first job was hedging and ditching which made me wonder why on earth I had joined the Land Army, but after getting over that things seemed easier.'

Pamela Castle comments on what a hard life it was when she started market gardening in Chippenham:

'I lived in a beautiful thatched cottage and my first job every day was pumping water in for the day. We then worked in the field, growing all vegetables but especially potatoes. There were also mushroom houses where we spent hours cutting and replanting mushrooms. In the winter there was hedging and ditching; standing up to our knees in muddy water always with leaky gumboots! When I had a free weekend I would cycle the 24 miles home on Saturday and back again on Sunday. This was the only way to get there and back in time. A very long and lonely ride over the Wiltshire downs.

I moved on after about a year to a lovely job, although still hard work, at Longford Castle near Salisbury.... The work was mostly in the greenhouses growing mainly tomatoes but also lots of other things including grapes and flowers. It was a very happy place. We spent long days out of season, scraping bark from the grape vines and getting them ready for the new season's crop. We picked hundreds of pounds of tomatoes and picked and bunched flowers. Also at Christmas we gathered lorry loads of holly and then wired it ready for holly wreaths. Very hard work on the hands. It was not all light work as we also spent days and weeks on the home farm on the cold and bleak downlands picking sprouts, cutting savoys, etc. It always seemed to be snowing at this time and we went along the rows removing the snow before picking. Most of the time it was so cold our hands were frozen and very painful. Tears were sometimes very near, but everybody sang while doing the jobs. A unit of airborne troops also shared a spot on the estate and kept us supplied with cups of hot tea. Sadly most of them went to Arnhem and did not return.'

Vera Wix was one of eight girls working on 'her' market garden:

'My nursery work continued and I then began to really enjoy it. I was liked it seemed, and got on well with the foreman and all the girls. I remember the first time I had to water a greenhouse the weight of the hose, but I soon got the hang of it. I said to the foreman, "I've finished that one". He said, "Get back in there, that wants three hours not one." We had to prove our salt and we all did. They, in the end, agreed we were useful and soon learnt the ropes.'

Still with those everlasting tomatoes—think how empty supermarket shelves would be today if only home-grown produce was available. Betty Cutts went to Wimborne in Dorset:

'... to grow tomatoes under glass, with heat. I shall never forget one day the foreman tore me off a strip because I left a door open that should have been closed. We were able to buy split tomatoes there at one shilling a large bag. The splitting is caused by over-watering. They don't get it today, in fact tomato growing of today has little in common with growing in 1940.'

Jo Greatorex went to Albourne, outside Hassocks, to grow fruit, potatoes, sprouts and of course, tomatoes. She remembers her stiffness after the first day. Mary Gerber says:

'Finally I made it to a form of market gardening at Peacehaven, fields of tomatoes, lettuce, radishes, peas, etc.'

Hilda Henderson worked in the grounds of another hospital—Wrekin Lodge:

'My billet was at the lodge with the stud groom and his wife and also another land girl, Elsie. We worked in the walled kitchen garden and on the farm going threshing, beet cutting, potato setting etc... I loved being in the gardens in the spring, it was a mass of blossom on the fruit trees....'

When Hilda finally arrived she found:

'There were large plots of ground which had to be dug by hand and planted with vegetables, and every morning we would go and gather the vegetables for dinner and then get to work to grow more.'

Audrey Manning, after training, felt ready to tackle any job though:

'I was sent to a market gardening farm with another land girl, Peggy. Along with the local women we packed lettuces, 24 to a box, pulled radishes, washed and tied them in bundles, packed rhubarb into boxes, and spent days at a time picking peas off the bines which had previously been pulled and left in huge piles.

One especially nice job was picking strawberries early in the morning before the sun was hot. We were paid piecework rates for this, so there was no time to eat more than an occasional strawberry. There was the onion field of course, where we spent weeks toiling away at some task or other, crawling along hand hoeing with sacking tied round our knees, then pressing the tops down, and later pulling them and laying them out for drying off, until they were ready for bagging up.

It was while we were working in this onion field when stopping for a brief rest one day, we saw the cows, in single file, going into the cowshed for milking. We were told each cow had a name and made her way to her own stall. We didn't believe cows could be so intelligent, but when next day we stood inside the cowshed to see for ourselves, the cows went berserk and charged out again refusing to enter until Peggy and I had gone!

With the coming of winter there were jobs to do of a different nature. Hedging and ditching was one of these, even in the pouring rain for we were issued with an oilskin and sturdy gumboots. Brussels sprouts covered in snow had to be picked, and when the weather was too bad, we mended boxes under cover.'

Joanna Murray spent her first year at a market garden at Llanishen on the outskirts of Cardiff:

'It was a very run-down place and I think the owner saw an opportunity of improving his lot by hiring out his land girls to work in the local residents' houses.... We used dreadful old bicycles to get to the places and he charged us a shilling a week for the use of them. After a while the girl I was in digs with and I rang the WLA HQ and complained that we were not doing war work, we were mowing lawns and growing flowers most of the time and... we were sent to Cannington, near Bridgwater, Somerset Agricultural College for one month to learn general farm work.'

Win Salter comments on the different outlook one acquires after knowing what goes into producing vegetables:

'When the war ended I returned to London but I couldn't pass a greengrocer's shop without thinking of the sacks of leeks I had dug in the rain and then carted on my back, or the Brussels sprouts picked on cold frosty mornings, not to mention the back aching job of picking runner beans grown in rows on the ground.'

15

THE TIMBER CORPS

The Timber Corps was a separate branch of the WLA, formed in 1942 when the blockade caused a shortage of timber. The structure and constraints of the WTC were the same as those for the WLA; girls volunteered from civilian life and were directed to where the need was greatest, sometimes with training and sometimes left to 'pick it up' (or saw it down) as they went along. There was not, however, the problem here of young girls being sent to isolated farms with all the attendant difficulties. And although the uniform was the same in most respects, the Timber Corps girls wore berets and different arm bands, the berets particularly being much envied.

It might be imagined that these girls were Amazonians, wielding axes and felling trees, and whilst they wielded and felled with the best, they themselves were not necessarily large and brawny. I attended an Essex WLA reunion and quite a high proportion of the girls were ex-Timber Corps—no, not the tallest or most muscular. For instance, I sat next to Enid Ballard who was 5ft 2in. in height and lightly built, who found the Timber Corps a satisfying life, as did the others.

Sheila McWilliam was stationed in Ballater and says that most of her workmates are now in their seventies with happy memories of their work together:

'There were twenty of us from Ballater and we cycled four miles every day to work. We had no training, just worked alongside the men and did what our bosses told us. The men cut down the trees and we did the snedding, which means chopping off the branches with an axe then peeling the bark off with a peeler, then sawing them into lengths which were required. After that we loaded the lengths which were mostly pit props onto a lorry then down four miles to Ballater station to load into the railway trucks for their destination.'

Elizabeth Anderson comments on the shared enjoyment:

'The work was very hard but we all enjoyed it—even during the winter when we often had to knock the frozen snow off the piles of pit props before loading them onto the lorries. Usually in February we had to burn the rows of brushwood which had been lopped off the felled trees during the dry season.'

Enid Ballard, who had been working in Marks and Spencer, chose the Timber Corps as a second option since the WRNS was not then recruiting:

'Arrived at the camp after travelling for 23 hours.... Did not sleep well, hard bed on three biscuits, as they called them. Old hut with stove in the middle. Had to take turns refuelling. Sent home for hot water bottle. Went by lorry into woods covered in snow. Had to take it in turns making sandwiches for the days in the woods. Quite a change from working in M & S office and stockroom! Just issued with Wellingtons and armband.... Most of the girls had colds so many in camp hospital. We never got warm. Food reasonable.... Started felling birch and sycamore trees, harder work than pines. Heard bombs exploding in Norwich.'

Joyce Whiteley also worked with a gang of girls:

'We worked under a foreman who organised us for the Ministry of Agruculture and Fisheries. We were paid 1s. 10d. per hour. Joan was a measurer for a gang of civilian fellers, going out every day in a bus with them. I was not long in the saw-mill before I joined a jolly gang of girls with whom I sawed pit props, felled, cleared small glades and made huge fires, until I left at the end of 1944.

One other job we did deserves a mention. It was called "brashing" and we were paid piecework rates. Brashing was the name given to the cutting down of acres of specially grown birch bushes. The twigs had to be cut to about a yard long, tied into neat bundles very tightly with sisal string, and earned us 3d. a bundle. I used to make about 17s. 6d. per day—quite a lot of bundles! They were used in the steel mills, thrown onto the sheets of hot metal, it seemed they smoothed out the bubbles and roughnesses very well. We were brashing on D-Day and felt we were very much a part of what was going on even though in a Lincolnshire wood!'

G. I. Ford had training in Suffolk:

'... and from there to Belford in Northumberland where we cut pit props. When we had snow in September we thought it was time to be a bit nearer home so put in for a transfer to Devon and from there I went to the Dulverton Sawmills and there I was classed as a sawyer.'

Alberta Gillatt trained in Weatherby, Yorkshire, for four weeks, with roll call outside at 6 a.m. and then to work on an open lorry:

'Worked from 7 a.m.-4.30 p.m. five days, from 7 a.m.-12 noon on Saturday.

Measuring felled timber, counting pit props, cords of wood, measuring brush burning, selecting telegraph poles, sawmill, work accounts and wages.... Worked with army, timber fellers and Italian POW... Had some hair-raising situations with the Italian POWs. Not so the German POWs, they kept their distance.'

16

PEST CONTROL

The words 'pest control' do not spring readily to mind as the most colourful section of the Land Army but nevertheless the girls took to it with their usual humour, in spite of parents' horror and a general disbelief that this was a suitable role for a woman.

L. P. Tuffs gives a picture of the rat catcher's duties and some of the hazards:

'When volunteers were needed for "Rat Catching" later named Vermin Destruction, I volunteered and after training and some experience was "ganger". We were given ordinary sugared bait to put down for a few days. This was cleared away after a day's lapse, poison bait was put in suitable rat runs, covered places. We returned early next day to collect the dead and remove any bait left. Where the infestation was bad or where it was unsuitable to use poison, Cyamag gas was used.

The method used for Cyamag was to firmly cover all found rat holes with soil or whatever, to insert the Cyamag pump hose into the biggest or easiest hole. One person used the pump, the rest stood round to kill off any escaping rats. Rats bolt out, they can jump a considerable distance, swim well in water, and can "turn face" if cornered, as I was soon to learn.

On one occasion we surrounded a small building in a field, the rats lived under the cement base. The farmer joined us with his dogs. We were all poised with various implements or sticks when the gas was pumped in. Several rats bolted at the same time, two in my direction. I chased and dealt with one but where was the other? Yes, it had climbed over my boot and up inside my dungarees. I shouted for someone to come, then shook the culprit to the ground. All those present bent down and pulled their socks over their trousers—the rat got away!'

We were all in one way or another involved in eliminating pests, particularly at harvest time when rats and mice were disturbed in their nests. Joy Enderby describes what happened on farms everywhere:

'We negotiated rats being thrown on the drum, I just used my pitch fork to eliminate them. On one occasion I had to have my hand covered in iodine—a smelly skunk was thrown up with one of the bales, iodine was the only thing available to get rid of the smell.'

I. Shepherd was a pest controller near Weston-Super-Mare:

'My job often called for a rat catcher at RAF Locking Camp. That was a very large aerodrome with civilians as well as flying crew. They frequently made fun of us saying things like: "Women weren't made for catching rats", and "How are you going to catch them?" The cookhouse was spotless but we could tell that there were plenty of them so we set about trapping them outside on the banks. The trick was to put the dead ones up our sleeves and place them behind cupboards while inspecting the premises. You have never seen such burly men move so fast down the corridor. They were the days!'

Humour rescued Lily Wightman from criticism:

'... I was transferred to Pest Control, living first in Settle Hostel then, when that closed living in "digs" in a cafe in Settle. My landlady was critical of the efforts of us land girls, so after a day spent collecting deceased rats I brought about 13 corpses back and arranged them in descending order of size on the doorstep and rang the bell. My landlady nearly fainted, but there was no more criticism of land girls.'

Mabel Potter also gives a graphic description of the rat catcher's job:

'We used to feed the rats for three days in farm buildings, fields etc. then starve them for one day, and on the fifth day put the poison down. Sixth day we collected the corpses, and unfortunately if the rats had dragged any of the poison outside their hole we used to get more than we bargained for in the odd dead hen or cat— most upsetting, especially for the farmers.'

Marion Powell recounts another hazard:

'While gassing rabbits with other girls we all fell asleep in the wood, the effects of the powder had got to us.'

There were, of course, two-legged pests and I received good advice during my training at Limpsfield, 'If in trouble, remember to bring up the knee sharply.' It worked! And presumably still does.

17
FLAX GROWING

Zelah Skinner, working in Ashford, Kent, was posted to flax factory:

'So Monday morning at 8 a.m. we reported for duty, there were other WLAs already working at the English Flax Co. Our work was outside in the factory grounds. Flax would be brought in from farmers who grew it, stacked in Dutch barns; there were three very large ones. Then when it was needed to go into the factory for threshing and processing we reloaded it on trailers and a tractor was always running around. So that and other jobs kept us busy for three parts of the year up until harvest time.

The factory itself was staffed with women, probably some local, also some who were evacuated from London. Also included were a few older men who generally helped outside with us, and a few village lads too young for call-up. We were rather a motley crew but all got on fine. The WLA girls came mostly from the south east, though I remember one from Wakefield, also from a variety of occupations.

Our first job was to reload a trailer of sheaves that had been capsized and most of the load was on the tarmac. After being given pitchforks which we eyed rather dubiously, we flexed our muscles, brutally attacked each sheaf and aimed them at the stacker who was a local man. He survived, as we did, but not without being on the receiving end of anti-WLA jokes. Here I should explain about flax. In peacetime the flax was, and no doubt still is, used mostly for linen, which made it such a strong and durable fabric. As far as I know flax was pre-war grown and processed in Ireland.

It is from the family of Linseed. The long narrow half inch or so pairs of leaves are the same, and the delicate five-petal light blue flower, but the length of the stem is far longer, up to probably forty inches in some crops. The stem is the producer of the fibre, that being the outer covering, "skin". The woody inside is knocked out in processing and the long tough silky fibre hanked, then baled at the factory. Then it was sent by rail probably to Ireland for the final processing ready for weaving. During wartime it was used, we understood, for aeroplane wing fabric and services' webbing equipment etc.

The whole cycle was as follows: the farmers who contracted to grow the flax were supplied with the seed—grew the crop which was periodically examined by "fieldsmen" (the experts from the factory). Then, when it was ready for harvesting, the WLA set forth around Kent and East Sussex with their equipment for the grand "pulling" season.

Pulling meant exactly that. Instead of flax being cut as corn was, it was pulled up from the ground by a series of thick rubber belts to get the full length of the stem and not to damage the fibre. Then steel "feeders" guided it into the binder where, at a certain weight, the "trip" operated the "knotter". And so the sheaves were tied and thrown out ready for the farmers to shock, and then stack ready for later in the year when lorries collected the crop and took it back to the factory. I "progressed" to a lorry latterly.

Some puller/binders were designed to be towed and powered by the Fordson tractors we travelled around with. There were also a few newly designed self-propelled pullers, rather weird creatures with a little engine in the front, up in the air. Behind that, lower down the binder was the pulling apparatus, and further back still, the driver's seat and controls. There was a seat alongside the binder in case the crop was a difficult one and an extra hand was needed to help the flax through. Otherwise the whole idea was that one person operated the complete system.

The pullers propelled by the tractors had the land girl driving and a farm hand sitting on the puller with an eye to the pulling/binding operation running smoothly. There were lots of hazards as there are with all machinery; one land girl caught her overalls on the power drive from the tractor to the puller and had them ripped off, to the delight of the farm lads. Another caught her hand in one of the rubber belts (at a guess now I would say they were about two inches wide and various lengths), her fingers, especially one, were permanently damaged even after extensive hospital treatment and skin grafts. So there was joy and tears.'

18

PIG FARMING

There's something risible about pigs, from whichever end you start viewing, together with a share of eccentric owners, as Joan Clifford found:

'I was sent to a farm owned by an old and very eccentric lady. I did not know it until later but I was to be her 26th land girl, and I stayed with her the longest, one year. She had two enormous sows—Luscious Lucy and Gracious Grace—though I had very different names for them! When I went to feed them one morning, they got out of their sty which was at the top of a large gorse field. It took me over an hour to get both of them back into the sty after running them up and down the hill and dodging in and out of the large gorse bushes.

One dark night at about 10 p.m. when I was having my nightly drink, my employer called for me to help get Lucy and about ten of her small piglets back into the sty, as they had forced themselves out and were loose in a field. She told me to pick up one of the little pigs which was still in the sty and she would find the sow and the others and drive them towards me. Knowing what Lucy was like when she had her young, I said, "She will go for me if she hears this one squealing." "No she won't," was the reply, so I did as I was told. The small pig was squealing blue murder and as the old sow came thundering towards the noise, I dropped the little one as the sow grabbed my leg, and I cleared a 5ft. 6in. fence as I'd never done before—nor since. My Wellingtons bore the teethmarks until the end of their days!

I had to drive this elderly lady into Banbury each week in a large old Austin-16 car, and this after driving a small Austin-7 van. I always had to dress up in my best full uniform for this duty. I soon realised why she couldn't keep her land girls and after an unforgettable year, I was transferred to another farm in the nearby village.'

Pigs, of course, were a valuable source of meat and all over the country swill was collected to eke out their food supply. Isabel Newnham had some experience of this:

'We had the contract to collect swill from an army camp not far away, twice a week. One day Jane and I went. She harnessed Nobby, the big carthorse, to the dungcart, put in the bins and away we went. I'm glad she did the driving as I wasn't used to horses. We reached the camp after a few catcalls from the kids in the school playground and some sniggers from passers-by.

There were squads of soldiers drilling on the parade ground, and instead of keeping to the road Jane drove straight between the ranks. The look on the faces of the soldiers was a study. They got redder and redder while they were trying not to laugh. It was at that moment that Nobby let us down. On the parade ground too! The soldiers roared and I laughed so much I fell backwards into the cart scattering the bins, while Jane was saying between her teeth, "Shut up Nobby, Nobby be quiet." When we reached the far side an officer came up and said, "Madam, you really must keep your horse under control..".... He let us off with a caution and we marvelled at the army discipline that enabled him to keep a straight face.... One soldier said, "Look, old Taffy's going to the seaside." We followed his gaze and saw Taffy walking sheepishly towards the parade ground with his bucket and spade.'

Doris Rowland found the work in the piggeries attached to Wye College hard, but enjoyable:

'There were two of us land girls who did all the heavy work, and a foreman in charge of us to do the office work. Our hours were from 7.30 to 5, with a day and a half off every other weekend. All the meal was mixed by us, by hand, the ingredients being emptied on the floor of the shed (approx 15cwt) and then turned by shovel three times. After this it was shovelled into 1-cwt sacks ready for use—nothing so small as ½-cwt sacks as there are today. A lot of barley meal was used in the mixes, and this came in 2½-cwt sacks. I became very proficient in balancing these sacks on my back with the opening over my right shoulder so that when I let go the meal would pour out quite easily, when I bent slightly forward. (Wouldn't like to try it today!)'

I have asked many land girls whether they were ever taught the right way to lift heavy weights but all have said no. Betty Venn too was sent to a piggery:

'... to the piggery after a lecture from the pig manager to be very careful the communicating doors were closed between breeds of pigs. Someone left one door open and all hell broke loose. The breeds got mixed, and did they fight, blood and squealing, it was terrible. The manager never did find the culprit. We had a few Gloucester Old Spots mostly kept for private use, but one day we took them to a perry orchard to eat all the fallen pears. Later on we walked through these orchards with barrels of this fruit which the pigs had got at, only to find the pigs were drunk, so with ropes we had to load them up and back to the farm—quite hilarious.'

And here's a round peg in a round hole. Joan Williams says:

'My most rewarding job was when I was asked if I would help out in the piggery. I had always said I didn't want anything to do with animals if I joined the WLA, but I ended up taking charge of 350 pigs and two boars and 15 sows. What hard work it was, but so interesting. I had to keep records of each sow and their litters, the piglets were fattened up for market—that was the only sad part of the job. I was allowed to enter some pigs and a sow in the Ashford show and won three first prizes.... They were some of the cleanest animals even though they say "dirty pigs".

19

CHICKEN FARMING

At the start of the war there were many poultry farms—not so many by the end since owners found that they were unable to keep going through lack of feed; egg consumption was reduced, powdered eggs being used instead. Meanwhile, as Isabel Newnham says:

> 'The Council started putting dustbins in the roads for people to put in their scraps and peelings. Every few days the bins were emptied into lorries and taken away to be boiled.... The lorry driver who brought it to the farm emptied the containers onto the shed floor and the "pudding" came out in great wads, the shape of the bins. We had to lever it apart with a spade before we could use it, and the things we found in it would even have ruined an elephant's digestion. There were rags, tins, string and cinders... then we had to add a little meal to it and mix it to a crumbly consistency with our bare hands and feed it to the poultry. The poor things hadn't done anything to deserve such treatment. I don't know if chickens can be sick but they looked a little pale about the wattles.'

Win Salter was posted to a poultry farm at Andover, Hants:

> 'It belonged to Major and the Hon. Mrs Bell and was a lovely place. Great big house built on a hill with acres of land divided into small fields each with a chicken house to house about 30 birds, all free range. At that time there were about 1,000 birds in all. I was to live with the family. After introductions I was taken round the farm by the Major and shown how to feel the bones in a chicken's back end to find out if it was laying! I was to be the only worker on the farm but for the first few weeks the present male employee would remain to show me how to feed the birds, muck out, water etc.... I found the work hard at first—a barrow load of chicken dung is surprisingly heavy.'

Joan Law too worked on her own but in rather different circumstances:

> 'I went to work at Oscott College where they train Catholic priests. It was like

being sent to Coventry. You couldn't speak to any of the young men. I worked mainly on my own with poultry and my best companion was a little dog.'

Mary Mallory's memories are painful for a different reason:

'I shall never forget dressing poultry until my fingertips bled, digging out snow drifts all day in order to feed the hens in a field, only to wake next morning to another heavy snowfall.'

However, Amy Johnstone found a silver lining:

'I landed down on this poultry farm in Fife where we hatched all these special chickens—doesn't sound much now but, thought it was hard work and long hours it was really interesting. I was so interested I married the boss after a few years!'

Mary Hall worked on a farm where most of the poultry were free range and had to be shut up at dusk.

'As we had the double summer time in operation I was often waiting for stupid hens to decide it was bedtime around 11 o'clock or so. Anyone who has had anything to do with hens will know they cannot be driven into their sleeping quarters, one has to wait (not always very patiently in my case!) for them to go into their huts of their own accord. Ducks and geese can be driven in so they didn't present any problem.'

Marjorie Harvey too, found shutting up the hens arduous but found a solution:

'... we took it in turns to do the poultry shutting up, except when we were at dances in the village when we both used to go up to the farm accompanied by various "soldiery", who thought it great fun to assist the land girls, until our boss's wife requested us to leave our boyfriends behind when shutting up the poultry.... Another weekly job was the killing, plucking and dressing of poultry—chickens, ducks and guinea fowl mostly, with the odd goose and turkeys at Christmas time. I didn't mind killing the chickens but I didn't like killing ducks.... The most vicious creature we had was the old gander who used to take a great delight in waiting until I was carrying two large buckets of water then sneak up on me and attack my legs. The beak of a gander can inflict some nasty bruises.'

Betty Venn, too, has something to say about killing the chickens:

'One day my partner Gwen was asked to kill a chicken, so she caught the chicken and chopped its head off. It got free, ran around the yard out of sight, so Gwen killed another, which did the same thing. The boss appeared just in time to stop the onslaught—I'm sure the boss could have wrung our necks too!'

Let Daphne Stone complete this:

'A girl sent by the local WLA headquarters had already started, and as she was some years older than myself, took precedence. She was perhaps an even more unlikely candidate than me, having worked as a lady's companion in North London, leading a rather sheltered life. Hence it was not surprising that she found it necessary to report the cockerels to our boss "for savaging the hens". (A misplaced blow for women's lib?).'

20

THATCHING

Although the word 'thatching' has a fine bucolic ring to it, not all the volunteers were altruistic, Jean Doe and Norah Golden for example. Jean writes:

'My friend Norah and I decided to apply for thatching and spar making, if only because thatching came in following hay-making and harvesting time but coincided with the two worst jobs—hoeing and potato picking! We passed our tests.'

and Norah says:

'Disliked spud picking so much—trained and qualified as thatcher and spar maker as this work coincided with the potato harvest.'

Maude Milliss also volunteered:

'The Warden asked for four volunteers to learn thatching—our hands shot up in unison!... We were transferred to Rednal on the Lickey Hills and a beautiful old house standing in acres of ground overlooking the Malvern Hills with a swimming pool in the garden. It belonged to the Cadbury (chocolate) family and I was to spend almost three happy years there.

We were taught to thatch ricks by a lovely old man. He never once lost patience with us although we couldn't have been the easiest of pupils. I thoroughly enjoyed it but only once was I called upon to thatch two ricks on my own for a local farmer. He was pleased with my work and I always remember the great feeling of achievement when I stepped back to admire the finished job—bright new straw gleaming in the sunshine all neatly pegged and clipped.

We didn't earn much (I believe it was around sixteen shillings a week) but it was sufficient for our needs, or I should say, mine, as there had never been a lot of money at home.'

Yvonne Timbs had a more peripatetic time:

'We were able to do a course of thatch making, using a large machine like a sewing machine using string and straw to make these mats. We were provided with a caravan and went from farm to farm making these mats. The farmers provided the straw and petrol for our engine, the Department towed us. We would be at each farm days or weeks, depending on how many stacks were to be thatched.'

Phyllis Munn describes how four girls worked together as a team:

'At Maidstone we had been given a brief period of training in the process of thatchmaking. This was a method of utilising straw for the purpose of protecting hay, which at that time was stored in stacks in the open. First, we clambered up the tall stacks and then threw down the bundles of straw. The straw was made into mats about four feet in length by means of a petrol-driven machine which produced two rows of stitching running through the centre. One girl stood at the table sifting out any rubbish, as only good straw made efficient mats.

The second girl operated the machine by means of a lever, while the other two cut the twine to the length required and rolled up the mats, tied them and stacked them in heaps ready for use. Other male farm hands did the actual thatching of the haystacks. After several weeks' work we had used all the straw and it was time to move on.'

21

FRUIT FARMING

Gladys Benton gives a vivid picture of fruit farming:

'Fruit picking time was really wonderful. First it was cherries, then the plums and apples and pears. There was a large barn, with a machine which sized and graded the apples, quite a new technique for those days. We all had to take our turn to work in the barn. None of us really liked this, because we would rather be out in the fields picking fruit.

At the end of the harvest Mr Carter would give all the staff a harvest supper in the village hall. This was quite something for wartime. Goose was always on the menu. Then we would sing and dance, and have a most enjoyable evening.

The autumn and winter months were spent pruning and spraying the trees. We were very fortunate to be one of the first farms in Britain to have its own pumping station for spraying. All the orchards had underground pipes with standpipes so many square feet apart, so we did not have to have tankers and it made spraying much easier.

I can remember one incident when we were spraying at the edge of an orchard. A regiment of soldiers were on a route march along the lane and the wind blew the spray over the hedge, covering them with this yellow substance (I cannot remember exactly what we were spraying). It may not have been funny for them, but the sight of all these yellow soldiers in disarray was something we laughed about for some time afterwards. We worked out in all weathers. I can remember 1944/45 being a really severe winter. We pruned the trees in a blizzard from 8 a.m. to 5.30 p.m. It was dark when we started and when we finished.'

Barbara Wickenden, too, takes us into the orchards:

'Picking apples from September 'til November. Pruning from then on, also grading and packing of apples when the weather was bad. Pruning continued 'til blossom time of cherries and plum trees. We had to shift ladders and boxes and climb trees. They were not kept as low as they are today.'

Marguerite Woodcraft had not only fruit trees but the everlasting hoeing to keep her busy:

'Acres and acres of fruit trees.... There was also celery to bank up and a spell of six weeks hoeing (I know not what), which I have never forgotten. My cousin and I had a pact as far as the fruit trees were concerned, when it was time for pruning them I chased the toads from under her tree and she used to prune the highest branches of mine.'

Joan Welbourn on the apple harvest:

'Sir Gerald Trevors was really good during the apple picking season—never did I imagine how apples had to be handled with great care.'

Barbara Ould transferred to fruit farming with Cadburys:

'It was much better as I had the company of seven other land girls. We all lived in this very large Georgian house with a lovely couple to look after us—we were known as the mad land girls—we probably were! It wasn't all lovely of course—one can remember really wicked cold mornings when just to stamp your feet on the hard ground nearly shattered your spine... and I well remember them using a single ploughshare to break the ground so that we could plant of all things—morello cherries. Every time I see a tin or fresh morello cherries, I can feel all that early morning frost.'

Sylvia Cawley too has icy memories:

'When winter came I called when it was 9 o'clock for our mid-morning cocoa— we were pruning in the orchard. I went to call out as usual and found my face and mouth had frozen stiff.

Summer was marvellous. I can remember during our mid-morning break lying under the apple blossom and seeing many Flying Fortresses in a blue sky, white trails behind. I thought of how peaceful it was on the farm and wondered what those bombers would be going into and if they would all come back. I don't take a sniff at apple blossom now without the memory of that day.'

22

SHEEP FARMING

Let Audrey Sykes paint an idyllic picture of the setting:

'There is nothing like the countryside in the very early morning, particularly in the summer, and one of my happiest memories is of my daily walk round the flock of sheep, to see that all was well after the night, no trouble from dogs or foxes and no sheep on its back and in danger of dying. Their ribs tend to spread if they lie on their backs for too long, and there is no way they can right themselves without help.

If they were in the meadow by the creek, it was an added bonus, especially if the tide was in. Sometimes there was a flat calm and complete and utter silence but for the sea birds and the lap of the water, then the distant sound of the tractors starting up, and signs of the farm awakening. The sun coming up, and the early light so clear, just to sit on a gate and listen was a perfect start to any day, and something I shall never forget.'

Audrey goes on to detail some of her duties:

'We had a flock of about 200 pedigree Southdowns and in January when it was very cold and wet the ewes would be brought into the yards for their lambs to be born. But sometimes we might find a near-frozen lamb born in a wet field, and this one would be taken into the farm kitchen, in front of the range fire and given milk and brandy from a bottle. It was surprising to see how quickly they recovered after that. There were occasional fatalities, and a dead lamb would be skinned, and the skin put on a twin lamb. The bereaved ewe usually accepted it as her own, after initial suspicion. Not all births were straightforward, with perhaps a lamb coming the wrong way, or maybe twins tangled up. My hands were smaller than Will's and I often got this job, with liberal applications of "green oil", an antiseptic lubricant, to try and unravel the knot. This was usually successful, but not always, and when it was impossible for the lamb to be born, the ewe would be killed and the carcase divided amongst the farm hands. My family were more than delighted to receive maybe a leg or a shoulder, but I found I could never face roast mutton, having known the animal intimately and "on the hoof", as it were.

One can become quite fond of sheep. We had two pedigree rams who became very aggressive towards one another after they were sheared, not recognising one another in their gleaming white undercoats, and they would butt each other, head on. As the warmer summer weather came, maggots were a great trial to sheep, the eggs being laid by the blow-flies all round the tail area. On hatching, the grubs proceeded to eat the animal alive if not caught in time. It was my responsibility to walk round the flock every day and look for restless stamping sheep, a sure sign of discomfort. If this was seen, they were cornered or hooked with a crook, and thrown. The wool was then snipped off with shears and strong disinfectant applied. Missing a sheep could result in large areas of flesh being eaten away. Nowadays the problem does not arise, as sheep are regularly dipped against scab and blow-flies, though by law we had to dip against scab. It was very important to throw the sheep the correct way, with their legs pointing away from the hand with the clippers.'

Betty Campbell echoes Audrey's words—'one can become quite fond of sheep':

'One of the nicer jobs was feeding the motherless lambs by the bottle. One in particular I'll never forget. He was a black-faced cross, and grew to be enormous. I named him Sammy. He must have thought he was a dog and followed me everywhere. It was quite annoying to be nearly at the village on my way to a dance, then to look round, and there he was. I was the laughing stock of my friends. The farmer shut him in the farthest field but still he arrived home. In desperation he had to be sold.'

May Readey enjoyed sheep-dipping and 'thrashing' days:

'The village bobby came to see that we were dipping the sheep correctly and workmen from neighbouring farms came to help with the thrashing. My job at sheep shearing was to turn the handle of the shearing machine and in between wrap up fleeces.'

And Brenda Golden managed eventually to amuse the farmer:

'There was one flock of sheep on the downs up towards Newlands Corner. The sheep were eventually sold off because of dog worrying. While culling and sorting them for sale one dived between my legs and I went for a short undignified ride backwards hanging on to the wool before slipping off inelegantly. That was the only time I ever saw the farmer laugh.'

Freda Smith took to her sheep with pride:

'I was sent to Beachampton Hall Farm to work for Mr Vesey... his speciality was Wiltshire horn sheep. He taught me how to get his sheep ready for a show, then I used to go with him to these shows. I have stood in the ring with three of his ewes at Northampton Sheep Fair Day and came away with first prize and a rosette—he was very pleased. I was able to shear a sheep in twenty minutes.'

Joan Turner learnt that not all rural jokes were just that:

'They told me to go in the field one morning and count the sheep. I didn't go straight away, thought they were trying to take the mickey out of me, but I had to go and they ended up looking for me.'

23

...AND AFTERWARDS

We've enjoyed looking back, remembering the girls we were, young and inexperienced. Those years have a special meaning for us and no matter how different we are one from another we have something in common. Some of the happiest of occasions are meetings of ex-land girls, full of laughter and understanding.

There is an official Land Army Association which has an annual reunion and there are many groups of 'girls' all over the country who have kept in touch, as Joan Williams says:

> 'When we left the hostel we made a pact that we would meet the first Sunday in October at 12 noon in five years time at Trafalgar Square. Nine of our gang turned up. Now we are all in our sixties we take it in turns to meet at one of our houses every year as our legs aren't so agile.'

Doreen Butler was in a hostel with 14 other girls:

> 'We still meet every year back where we were stationed, still in touch with farmers and workers. They join us in our get-togethers.'

Some have kept in touch with landladies and farmers. Betty Ambler says:

> 'I went to one farm mostly and I have kept in touch with them ever since. We have gone for holidays when my children were young and they never wanted to go to the seaside; they always wanted to go to the farm.'

Julia Porteous regards her landlady, Mrs Wharrie, as a mother figure:

> '...she is still alive and is 86 years old. We often have her down to stay with us.'

Jane Rooke kept in contact with every landlady she had and still writes to a dear couple who call her 'our gal'. (Jane is 71). Yvonne Timbs (now in New South Wales) still has links with her landlady.

Although, like everyone else, we dreamed of an end to war, the reality of 'civvy' life came as a shock to some. Betty Arbon comments on the way we left:

> '...we had to hand in our uniform, why I will never know. We were allowed to keep our greatcoats, armbands and shoes. The rest had to go in exchange for 20 clothing coupons. The "Cinderella Army". We did not receive any gratuity and jobs were difficult to find.'

As Hilda Henderson says, being indoors was very hard at first:

> '...my mother suggested I took an allotment just over the road where we lived. It caused a stir among elderly gardeners who worked there, they kept walking past to watch me work.'

Maude Milliss too continued to enjoy outdoor work:

> '... it gave me a liking for gardening which has grown over the years. My husband and I grow all our own vegetables and flowers from seed, and I spend many happy hours tending my plants, often reminscing over the happy days spent at Spinneyfield.'

Margaret Collyer was another who never went back indoors:

> 'I enjoyed my time in the Land Army and learned a lot which came in very handy when I married a farmer. I still love the life and at over 70 years I still have my ponies. I breed Shetland ponies and have two retired riding horses, one 30 and the other 33 years, so my days are full looking after them.'

Some of us have revisited the scenes of those hard working years, not always happily, as D. Heppell says:

> 'I returned to these places a few years ago. My daughter took me by car. It was a shock to me as I expected to find the farms and buildings as they were all those years ago. I'm afraid they were dilapidated and falling apart like one sees old farm buildings—not a pretty sight after spending some hard working and happy years there.'

Jo Burton found no signs of the hostel where she lived, it is now part of a huge housing estate on the outskirts of the town. A compensation, however:

> 'My two grandchildren are always enchanted with my tales of "granny in the war".'

Norah Welburn found:

'Where the hostel stood they've built an old people's home and the lady whose farm we stayed at lives there.'

Mabel Potter obviously retained her sense of humour:

'I eventually married a Cheshire man who turned out to be a greengrocer in civvy street, so I was still associated with potatoes. Now at 70 years of age all I do is eat them!'

For Audrey Sykes the sight of 'her' farm brought sadness:

'After Old Goodger died, the farm was let again and the new tenants promptly pulled out all the hedges, widened the gateways and filled in the ditches. All the animals were sold, hence no dung for the fields, only cereals being grown, which are "encouraged" to bigger and better crops by the liberal application of nitrates. When I last saw them the piggeries and cowpen and stables too were falling down. The paths were full of brambles. I heard that the whole complex was to be demolished to make way for a housing estate. The farm as I knew it is no more, and what is left behind is without soul and character. How Goodger would have hated to see the land he loved and cared for brought to this, when in the years I knew it we won prizes for the best kept farm in the area.'

C. B. Davenage sees a different farming world from the one we knew:

'When I see farming today, with huge fields with the hedges all removed.... Every field had a name and you knew exactly where you were working, we knew the names of all the cows, everything is so mechanised.... The work was very hard and I am sure there are many who still suffer as a result of the hours spent in the cold and wet, working whatever the weather every hour of daylight, doing manual labour for which I think we were not given sufficient recognition or credit when the war ended. I myself suffered with my hands for many years and also have arthritis now.'

Audrey Bagnall, however, was able to make use of her skills:

'... my next door neighbour leaned over the garden wall and asked if I could help him with his newly acquired goat. His wife was out for the day and he had tried to milk the goat but could get nothing. I told him that I knew very little about goats and had never milked one, but I used to be able to milk a cow. So working on the principle that a goat is like a cow—only smaller and fires on half as many cylinders—I went round to make the acquaintance of "Twinkle". With a little talking to, a bit of patting, a pan of feed for her and some nice warm water to wash her udder, I got down to the job of milking her. My neighbour was quite impressed when the first squirts of milk started coming into the pail. "Twinkle" and I both gave a sigh of relief, I felt the years roll back, the milk came freely in a rhythmic duet frothing into the pail. It is forty-five years ago since I learnt to milk, I remember it all as if it were yesterday.'

Betty Jackson has donated all her WLA memorabilia to the Museum of Lincolnshire Life, but still has her memories:

'Later my daughter was christened at Thornton Church. Molly the land girl who got married at Thornton Church in 1942 returned there 24th April 1990, I returned again in October and saw that she and her husband had signed the visitors book, but alas there was no address.'

The indefatigable Audrey Wiitta wrote to the Ministry of Defence saying 'what about a medal?' Officially, of course, we didn't carry arms, unofficially we were dab hands with a pitchfork should the need arise! However, Audrey had an answer to her query, enclosing a claim form DM2 for the Defence Medal for which a minimum of three years should have been served. This reply came from:

Constitutional (A) Division,
Home Office,
Queen Anne's Gate, London SW1H 9AT

There is, however, another example of care—the WLA Benevolent Society was set up in 1942. Some 18,000 members benefitted but by 1981 the fund had shrunk so much that the small sum still remaining was remitted to the Family Welfare Association. Mrs J. Dixon, the Grants Officer at the FWA is sympathetic to ex-WLA members and any requests for assistance should be addressed to her at:

The Family Welfare Association,
501–505 Kingsland Road,
Dalston, London E8 4AU

The Scottish WLA Benevolent Fund is, however, still in existence although funds are small, and is adminstered by:

Mrs Doreen Butler,
5 Lorne Terrace,
Lochgilphead, Argyll.

Some recognition has come too. Salisbury Cathedral has a stained glass window showing land girls: we appear too on the D-Day tapestry shown in Portsmouth; there are idealised pictures on posters etc. of land girls looking clean and tidy, wearing woollies, carrying sheaves of corn; but perhaps best of all is a plaque in Devizes, Wilts. put up by farmers grateful for the work done by land girls. The Imperial War Museum holds contributions from land girls and there are doubtless other acknowledgements up and down the country.

Joan Clifford has summed up her Land Army days for an entry for the mini-saga and has given me permission to quote:

> 'London to an Oxfordshire farm. Hard work—long hours—little pay.
> Charged by horse—bitten by sow—recaptured escaped bull and two large sows.
> Bolting horse—births and deaths. Working alongside POWs.
> Happy, sad, hilarious, miserable, dangerous, wet, hot, cold, but memorable days.
> I married the farmer!'

So here's to all ex-land girls, the farmers who employed them, the landladies who cared for them—a mixed bag of memories but we look back with pride.

FURTHER READING

Women in Uniform. Jane Waller and Michael Vaughan-Rees. Papermac. Chapter 5.

Unsung Heroines: The Women who won the War. Robin Cross and Jenny de Gex. Sidgwick and Jackson. Chapter 4.

Women on the Land: Their story during two world wars. Carol Twinch. Lutterworth Press.

The History of the Second World War: Agriculture. K. A. H. Murray. HMSO.

The Women's Land Army. V. Sackville-West. Michael Joseph.

War in the Countryside 1939–45. Sadie Ward. David and Charles.

Poems of the Land Army: An Anthology of Verse. V. Sackville-West. The Land Girl, 1945.

Ourselves in Wartime. Various. Odhams Press Ltd. pp139–143.

Meet the Members: The Timber Corps of the WLA. Bennett Brothers, 1944.

Wartime in Kent 1939–40. Meresborough Books, 1990.

If Their Mothers Only Knew. Shirley Joseph. Faber & Faber.

ACKNOWLEDGEMENTS

I am grateful to all those who have helped to compile this book. Nearly 300 former land girls answered my appeals in the press or on the radio, to all of whom I owe my thanks. The following have been quoted directly:

Irene Abbott; Billie Alexander; Irene Algie; Betty Ambler; Elizabeth Anderson; Molly Andrew; Betty Arbon; Agnes Aspinall; Audrey Bagnell; Christine Bailey; Joan Baker; Enid Ballard; Cynthia Banbury; Jean Barnes; Marjorie Beasley; Mary Becraft; Enid Bennell; Gladys Benton; Margot Bettles; Ann Bibbings; Jo Bicknell; Olive Black; Daphne Blanford; Caroline Blyth; Margaret Bodman; Chris Breeze; Eva Briley; Marie Brockett; Vi Bromley; Dorothy Brook; Audrey Bruton; Jo Burton; Doreen Butler; Vera Calf; Betty Campbell; Molly Campbell; Vera Campbell; E. V. Campion; Pamela Castle; Sylvia Cawley; Dorothy Chard; Joan Clifford; Margaret Collyer; Phyllis Collyer; Dorothy Coonrod; Phyllis Corry; Joan Coulson; Margaret Coulson-Loam; Pam Crellin; Enid Dalloway; C. B. Davenage; Jean Dawe; Sylvia Dawn Cawley; W. M. Debenham; Pat Detry; Jean Doe; Elsie Druce; Joy Eichler; Kathleen Ellis; Jean Emerson; Joy Enderby; Violet Farrant; G .l. Ford; Gladys Foster; Barbara Fowler; Dorothy Fox; Vera Gaskell; Julie Gazy; Peggy George; Maisie Geraerts; Lilian Gerber; Alberta Gillatt; Jessica Godwin; Brenda Golden; Norah Golden; K. Golder; Sheila Gordon-Rae; Elinor Grant; Pauline Grant; Joy Greatorex; Frances Gregg; M. Griffin; Doris Hall; Margaret Hall; Mary Hall; Elizabeth Hanmer: Dorothv Harmer; Marjorie Harvey; Joan Hawell; Norah Hawkes; Molly Hefford; Hilda Henderson; D. Heppell; Rene Hillier; Marion Hinckley; Myra Hobden; Mary Horrobin; Esme Hotchkiss; Joan Howell; Betty Jackson; Marjorie James; Daphne Jauncey; I. Jeffery; Evelyn Jenkin; Nancy Johnson; Amy Johnstone; Ruby Jones; Freda Kerley; Ribby Killick; Joan Law; Hilary Lawn; Gwen Lawrence; Joy Lawrence; Gladys Levingbird; Doreen Liebrandt; Angela Lincoln; Gloria Lombardo; May Love; Jane McLaren; Kathleen McManus; Connie McNichol; Sheila McWilliam; Mary Mallory; Audrey Manning; Joyce Mayhew; Maude Milliss; Ivy Mooney; Joy Morgan; Joyce Murphy; Joanna Murray; Rose Motherdale; Phyllis Munn; Marjorie Nesfield; Isabel Newnham; Jean Oglethorpe; Laura Oliver; Betty Otway; Barbara Ould; Olwen Owen; Joyce Palmer; I. Pamphlett; Vivienne Passmore; Brenda Penfold; Olive Pettitt; Mary Phipps; Julia

Porteous; Joyce Porter; Mabel Potter; Diana Powell; Marion Powell; Irene Poulter; M. Price; Doreen Rapley; May Readey; Vera Redshaw; Theo Rice; Enid Roffey; Jane Rooke; Marjorie Rossi; Doris Rowland; Win Salter; Joyce Sansom; Betty Schibler; Joan Shakesheff; L. Shepherd; Helen Sheppard; Joyce Sherman; Marjorie Short; Clara Sibley; Dorothy Simpson; Gladys Sirs; Zelah Skinner; Freda Smith; M. Smith; Win Smith; Daphne Stone; Audrey Sykes; Ailsa Tanner; L. G. Thompson; Yvonne Timbs; Olga Tremayne; L. P. Tuffs; Joan Turner; Betty Venn; Elizabeth Venner; Mary Vickery; Evelyn Waight; Vera Wakeling; Ivy Walker; Pat Warren; Marjorie Waterhouse; Branwen Weekes; Joan Welbourn; Norah Welburn; Phyllis Westaway; Phyllis Weston; Joyce Whiteley; Barbara Wickenden; Lily Wightman; Audrey Wiitta; Win Wild; Joan Williams; Mabel Williams; Vera Wix; Ellen Wood; Marguerite Woodcraft; Joan Wright; Barbara Youngman.

LIST OF ILLUSTRATIONS

32. Courtesy of Jonathan Reeve JR1759b92pic7 19391945.

33. Courtesy of Jonathan Reeve JR1788b92pic36 19391945.

34. Courtesy of Jonathan Reeve JR1789b92pic37 19391945.

35. Courtesy of Jonathan Reeve JR1770b92pic18 19391945.

36. Courtesy of Jonathan Reeve JR1757b92pic5 19391945.

37. Courtesy of Jonathan Reeve JR1792b92pic40 19391945.

38. Courtesy of Jonathan Reeve JR1768b92pic16 19391945.

39. Courtesy of Jonathan Reeve JR1864b93p59 19391945.

40. Courtesy of Jonathan Reeve JR1772b92pic20 19391945.

41. Courtesy of Jonathan Reeve JR1773b92pic21 19391945.

42. Courtesy of Jonathan Reeve JR1774b92pic22 19391945.

43. Courtesy of Jonathan Reeve JR1860b93p34 19391945.

44. Courtesy of Jonathan Reeve JR1868b93p90BR 19391945.

45. Courtesy of Jonathan Reeve JR1859b93p33 19391945.

46. Courtesy of Jonathan Reeve JR1752b92p112 19391945.

47. Courtesy of Jonathan Reeve JR1765b92pic13 19391945.

48. Courtesy of Jonathan Reeve JR1799b92pic47 19391945.

49. Courtesy of Jonathan Reeve JR1769b92pic17 19391945.

50. Courtesy of Joan Mant.

51. Courtesy of Joan Mant.

52. Courtesy of Joan Mant.

Illustration on page 22 Courtesy of Jonathan Reeve JR1754b92pic2 19391945.

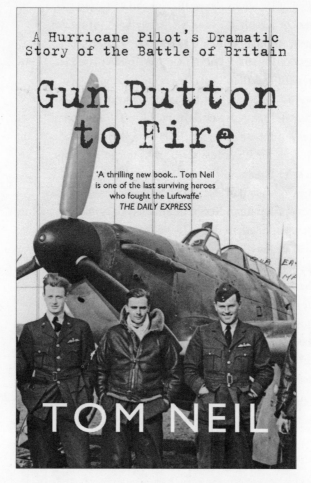

Also available from Amberley Publishing

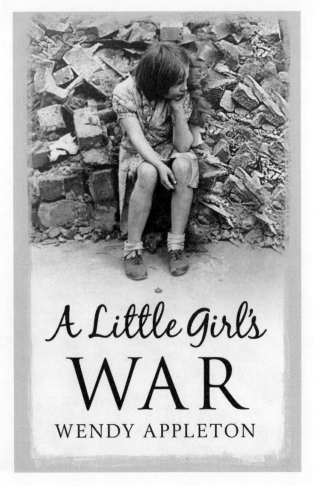

From the London Blitz to Burnley as an evacuee

'Few people write with affection about their time as evacuees, but that is what Wendy Appleton has done in her charming memoir' THE DAILY MAIL

Wendy ran home through the streets of Bexleyheath with the air-raid siren wailing, her little gas mask box bumping against her hip. Just as she reached her front gate, a Spitfire spiralled out of the air and crashed into the school field at the end of the road. You never forget a moment like that.

Wendy Appleton describes beautifully the memories that were imprinted so deeply on her young mind. These pages contain the sights, songs and sounds of her wartime childhood.

£9.99 Paperback
128 pages
978-1-4456-0639-2

Available from all good bookshops or to order direct
Please call **01453-847-800**
www.amberleybooks.com

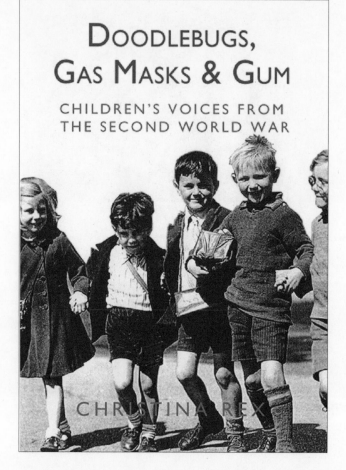

Also available from Amberley Publishing

A fabulous slice of wartime nostalgia, a facsimile edition of the manual used by the Land Girls during the Second World War

'Fascinating... gives a good insight into the history of he WLA'
BBC WHO DO YOU THINK YOU ARE MAGAZINE

First published in 1941, *Land Girl* was a practical guide for the city slickers who were recruited into the Women's Land Army and sent to work on farms in the English countryside to replace the men who had joined up. An amazing period piece, hundreds of thousands of copies were printed and sold and it became one of the year's best-selling books.

£9.99 Paperback
25 illustrations
160 pages
978-1-4456-0279-0

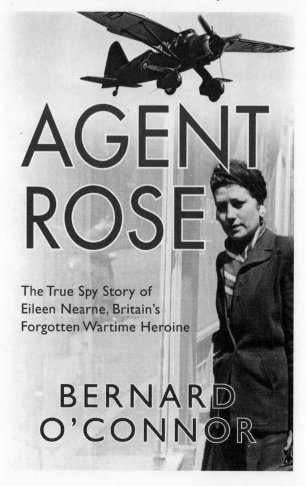

Available September 2012 from Amberley Publishing

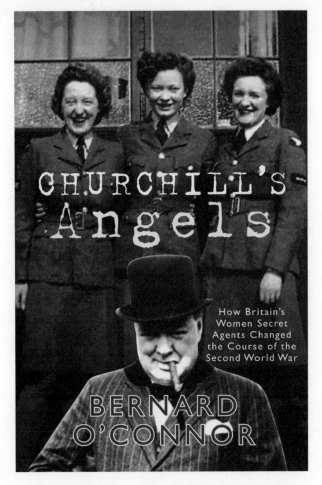

The story of Britain's bravest women

Over 70 female agents were sent out by Britain's Special Operations Executive (SOE) during the Second World War. Bernard O'Connor relates the experiences of these agents of by drawing on a range of sources, including many of the women's accounts of their wartime service. There are stories of rigorous training, thrilling undercover operations evading capture by the Gestapo in Nazi-occupied France, tragic betrayals and extraordinary courage.

£20 Hardback
30 illustrations
288 pages
978-1-4456-0828-0

Available September 2012 from all good bookshops or to order direct
Please call **01453-847-800**
www.amberleybooks.com

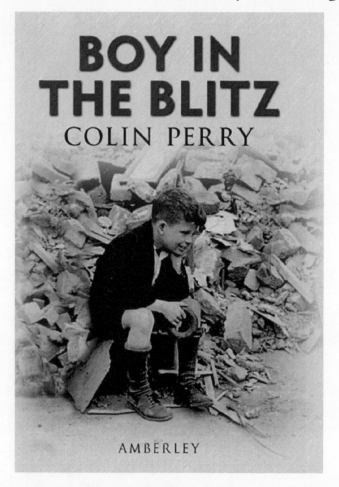

Also available from Amberley Publishing

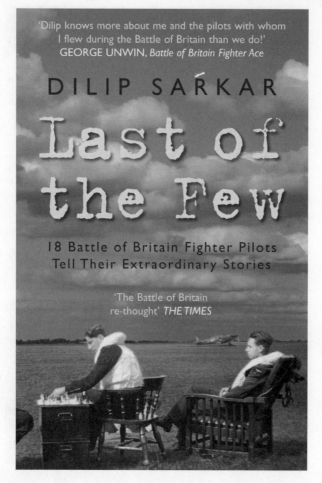

'Dilip knows more about me and the pilots with whom
I flew during the Battle of Britain than we do!'
GEORGE UNWIN, *Battle of Britain Fighter Ace*

DILIP SARKAR

Last of
the Few

18 Battle of Britain Fighter Pilots
Tell Their Extraordinary Stories

'The Battle of Britain
re-thought' *THE TIMES*

*18 Spitfire and Hurricane fighter pilots recount their experiences
of combat during the Battle of Britain*

'Dilip knows more about me and the pilots with whom I flew during the Battle of Britain than we do! If
anyone ever needs to know anything about the RAF during the summer of 1940, don't ask the Few, ask
him!' GEORGE 'GRUMPY' UNWIN, Battle of Britain fighter ace

£9.99 Paperback
55 Photographs
224 pages
978-1-4456-0282-0

Available from all good bookshops or to order direct
Please call **01453-847-800**
www.amberleybooks.com